Dear Coach Liz,

Thank you for being such a monumentally important part of my journey. When I realized I needed change you popped into my

FAR BETTER

LIFE. I don't believe in randomness ♡ Can't wait to see what we conquer together next!

Thanks For Being you ♡

Miranda

www.amplifypublishing.com

Far Better: Self-Discovery through the Power of Endurance Sports

The information in this book is meant to supplement, not replace, proper endurance sports training. Like any sport involving speed, equipment, balance, and environmental factors, racing poses some inherent risk. The author and publisher advise readers to take full responsibility for their safety and know their limits. Before practicing the skills described in this book, be sure that your equipment is well maintained, and do not take risks beyond your level of experience, aptitude, training, and comfort level.

For more information, please contact:
Amplify Publishing, an imprint of Amplify Publishing Group
620 Herndon Parkway, Suite 320
Herndon, VA 20170
info@amplifypublishing.com

Library of Congress Control Number: 2023903660

CPSIA Code: PRV0923A

ISBN-13: 978-1-63755-331-2

Printed in the United States

I can never convey my gratitude for the amount of love, support, and encouragement I have received from Jamie, my supportive partner, who has provided a consistent and unwavering belief that I am capable of doing anything I put my mind to. He has also called out my bullshit from day one, and our relationship is integral to my continued growth and learning—and ultimately accepting myself enough to write this book. I thank him and my children for loving me as I am.

FAR BETTER

SELF-DISCOVERY THROUGH THE POWER OF ENDURANCE SPORTS

MIRANDA BUSH

amplify

an imprint of Amplify Publishing Group

CONTENTS

INTRODUCTION

DARE MIGHTY THINGS

Far better it is to dare mighty things, to win glorious triumphs,
even though checkered by failure, than to take rank with those poor
spirits who neither enjoy much nor suffer much, because they live in
the gray twilight that knows neither victory nor defeat.
THEODORE ROOSEVELT

MY LOCAL TRIATHLON TEAM adopted "Dare Mighty Things" from Roosevelt's quotation as our motto in 2017, when I coached and led our largest contingency of athletes yet to the goal of completing Ironman Wisconsin. One of our most charismatic and vocal members suggested the quote, and immediately the team's co-owner, Kelli, and I agreed it represented our team perfectly.

For most of the first-timers, in 2017, to "dare mighty things" meant bravely taking on the ominous Ironman race goal and completing it to the best of their abilities. At the time, I believed it was the same for me. Since that race, it has personally taken on a different meaning: now to "dare mighty" means cultivating awareness of how I am ever evolving and growing as a human through the highs and lows of life. It means showing up for hard things, even when they seem impossible. And it means learning to love people more through seeing, hearing, and knowing both myself and them. I have been able to incorporate the "far better it is to dare mighty things" philosophy into my life in order to authentically show up for myself, my goals, and my relationships. I will never arrive at perfection, but I do sincerely try to be present every single day in my one big, beautiful, messy life.

I know we are all born fully worthy, even if the road to this way of thinking has been filled with potholes. My parents, who were very young when they had me, modeled confidence and nurtured my worth from birth. They brought my brothers and I into this world with what I am sure started as a "fake it until you make it" boldness that grew into real trust in their own capabilities. My parents were hardworking, risk-taking entrepreneurs who were well respected by their small community. I always saw them as "edgy" in their decision-making, which rebelled against the standards of where and when I grew up—from my mom's fashion and home-decor choices to my dad tending our extra-large garden in the height of the processed convenience foods era. When I look back, I now see how these choices represented a deeper sense of freethinking, confidence, and willingness to challenge cultural expectations. They have encouraged and still do encourage me to do the same, loving and accepting me through my rebellious years and as an imperfect adult.

Whether or not I always saw it or relied on it, I am thankful I have had the support to evolve without overly questioning this foundational worthiness. The youthful and teen parts of my journey were spent in a mostly self-serving existence, cultivating a lifestyle that allowed me to be in control, disrespect my goals, and often not honor my body. I considered myself an athlete, participating in organized baseball as a young girl and then volleyball and basketball in high school. And I always jumped at the chance to play pickup football and baseball games with my brothers. But I know now that many factors in and outside myself contributed to my fear of going "all in" as an athlete, or really in anything I pursued at a young age. Through these years, my confidence slipped away and eventually morphed into a false sense of pride I carried into college and early into my marriage. Covering my insecurities with this bravado-type faux confidence led me to make many choices that harmed myself and others and eventually led to my desire for change. Thankfully, I could still return to my foundation of loving grace and unwavering support, and it inspired me to learn how to navigate these perceived failures and return to getting to know myself more honestly and authentically. I was able to resurface my belief in my worthiness and trust that all the hurdles in my journey needed to be hopped over, crawled under, or toppled in order for me to be exactly where I am today. I have learned that repressing parts of our lives to forget does not serve our growth process; we must accept, heal, and learn. And it must be done with a hearty serving of grace, with the understanding that we are likely to fall into some default patterns of behavior. And that's okay.

We can benefit from not focusing on the past, but instead use gained wisdom to live in the present.

As I live each day in this world, self-discovery through my coaching career and my racing hobby continue to be vital to my personal growth and development. Through years of experience and reflection, I have learned that the process of training for an endurance event closely mimics the work needed to reach a state of understanding oneself.

Going far can help us ultimately find our way back to ourselves.

In addition to helping us be more fully alive as humans, I believe the mental side of training is best built on a foundation of self-awareness. Participating in endurance sports became my way of investing more in myself and bringing the lessons to others in a relatable way—through coaching, speaking, and writing. I continue to grow as an athlete and coach while also learning more about myself as a human. Eventually, my eyes were opened further to the cultural messaging and conditioning that continue to influence me in all aspects of life, including goal setting. My experience in the fitness industry has shown me that we can all benefit from practicing self-compassion, awareness, and acceptance by supporting others and also by educating ourselves and others on the impact of outside influences in order to live a fully authentic life. Living this life is the way to go forth and create change for all humanity.

The personal lessons I have learned through the lens of coaching, training, racing, and health coaching are invaluable to me, and I hope you can learn from them as well. Participating and working in race training, as well as general fitness and wellness, have provided a conduit of hope to so many people, and many of these people have been essential to my own self-discovery. I have learned much from my relationships with coaches, mentors, mentees, athletes, friends, family, gym members, and strangers. I have provided guidance and learned from these relationships, and even though some of them have fallen away, others are lifelong bonds. The thoughts in this book are my connections made through all my life and racing experiences. I am a professional triathlon and health coach, but I am most certainly not a psychologist, nor am I pretending to be one. I highly suggest working with trained professionals within those areas of expertise.

HOW DID I GET HERE?

In 2008 I toed the start line of my first half-Ironman: the Pigman Triathlon, (somewhere) in Iowa. Even if the exact Midwest location is a bit fuzzy, the memory of the swim portion of the race will likely always remain vivid. We all looked the part: wet suit–clad bodies, gender-specific race-issued swim caps, and goggles perched on our heads. But as I stood in the corral with other nervous and excited triathletes ready to take on the race, I couldn't help but wonder, *How did I get here*? I had trained for months, and this triathlon was a vital part of my plan to conquer Ironman Wisconsin 2009. But although I had the outward look of a seasoned triathlete, part of me still felt like an imposter.

Through a process of perseverance, I had learned how to swim for endurance just the year before. So, when I exited the water at 1.2 miles around forty-three minutes later, my elation was clear in my giant smile. I was excited but also still surprised I had truly conquered that goal. I went on to ride the 56-mile cycling course at a respectable clip. I was still inexperienced on the bike, but after training with some tough cyclists—mostly male, but a couple of badass females as well—I felt confident in my capabilities. When I got to the run, however, the only way I can describe it is that I completely and utterly fell apart.

It was hot, and I felt like I was literally going to melt on to the asphalt. I casily succumbed to long bouts of walking while complaining to anyone who would listen along the way. I made myself a victim of the weather. Looking back, I know I hadn't consumed the best nutrition for my body and definitely hadn't taken in enough fuel or fluids. Some of my problems were truly due to straight-up triathlon inexperience, but the way I reacted to the task at hand was also duc to a lack of practice handling adversity in my life. In much of my young adulthood, I had often walked away or blamed others when things didn't go my way, making excuses and finding a way to make myself a victim. So that day I had my arsenal of excuses readily available—the proof that I was incapable of performing to the best of my ability. I couldn't connect with my own body and experience, because I had gotten so far away from knowing and trusting *me*. And when I crossed the finish line, I promptly decided I couldn't have done any better, and it "wasn't my fault."

I realize now that I spent many years disconnected from my body, and often disassociated in my thinking. And I distinctly remember one of my first moments of awareness starting to creep in. Roughly four years after my first triathlon, I was sitting in the Oregon High School Performing Arts Center awaiting the start of my only daughter, Halle's, fourth-grade orchestra concert. I looked around at all the parents eagerly anticipating the arrival of the young musicians, with smartphone cameras poised to capture every moment. As the kids of near middle-school age lugged the classical instruments onto the stage, my husband, Jamie, and I waved vigorously to Halle. She smiled and attempted to wave back without dropping her enormous cello. The lights in the audience dimmed, and the tiny Yo-Yo Ma wannabes prepared to play their first note.

I had the most overwhelming and nearly frightening thought: *How did I get here?*

I was well aware I had arrived at Oregon High School willingly via our own car, driven by Jamie. I am referring to the sudden realization that I had an eleven-year-old daughter (and ten- and nine-year-old sons). I was shocked that I was adult enough to have rented a cello and taken Halle to school every day to have the opportunity to play the rented cello. I had fed her, clothed her, and helped her grow and flourish. And then, what felt like mere hours later, she was suddenly capable of playing in an orchestra. I recognized that I could (and can) be a bit dramatic in my thinking, especially in contrast to my husband's pragmatic style, but in that moment I was internally tormented. How *did I* get to this place in my life? I leaned over and whispered this question to Jamie, and he replied, "I know. Time is going so fast." I shrugged and turned to watch the show, still reveling in the disbelief that it was actually happening. Although I was smiling so hard that my face hurt, I couldn't shake this feeling that I was an imposter in the crowd. I absolutely loved my kids and spent most of my time making sure all their needs and wants were met, but I just couldn't believe this was possible.

Six years later, after completing many triathlons and marathons and having many parenting (and other) opportunities to gain life wisdom, I found myself having a similar thought process during a different experience. One morning I rolled over at 4:50 a.m. after a fitful night's sleep—at this age, involving two night sweats. I decided there was no possible way I could go to the pool for the 5:30 a.m. lap swim—I was just too tired and would most likely sink to the bottom and drown if I even tried. I picked up my phone, reset my alarm for 6:00 a.m., and cuddled up with Jamie for one more perfect hour of sleep. Twenty minutes later, I was driving to the pool with my suit on under my sweatpants, thinking, *How did I get here*? Even though it was what some people would call an ungodly hour to be out and about, I knew I had gotten dressed willingly in my own bathroom, brushed my teeth, and driven my car out of our garage. But the process that went into it surprised me for a moment: I had thought I was snuggled in for one more hour of rest—most certainly an hour that would have made the biggest difference in the productivity of my day—but I had goals, and I knew I could swim without literally sinking to the bottom of the pool.

Later, while swimming, I had the same thought in yet another context. While I was taking a scheduled rest, I looked to see several friends, teammates, and the other characters who populate the pool every Monday, Wednesday, and Friday at 5:30 a.m. *How did I get here*? I marveled at the fact this was an accepted norm for me: a girl who grew up with no indoor pool and could swim to stay alive, but not more than one lap consecutively. The puzzlement I had felt six years prior while watching Halle in the orchestra was replaced with an amazing amount of gratitude.

Later still, while on a run—when my head's out of the water, it is easier to think—I was able to reflect further on the question recurring throughout my life: *How did I get here*? I captured it and dissected it, questioning what made my brain produce this thought again as well as why I would entertain the idea that I was an imposter and that life was something "that just happened to me." In the past, I had floated through life, blowing with the wind, along for the ride. Life was going to take me wherever it pleased. I believed in God's timing and pretended that questioning my trajectory would be doubting his plan. But although my faith is the foundation I have always stood upon, I was making it merely something I was hiding behind in order to not take charge of connecting wholly to myself. I had been reacting to life, making many beautiful memories and enjoying so many grateful moments, but still not connected to my body and experiencing all the vulnerability of being fully human.

That Ironman race in 2017 was pivotal for me in my life as an athlete, coach, and overall as a person. But looking back, I can see that my training and racing journey had already been a catalyst for building a more solid mental and emotional foundation. Although I was not fully aware of the process, I was learning how to evolve by understanding and accepting more of what it means to be *human*. I was developing a more heightened body, mind, and spiritual awareness. My journey of covering many miles was actually putting my feet on a path to myself.

I was able to recognize that disconnecting from myself has been holding me back from living a full, authentic life.

I had all my worth inside me, but I wasn't showing the world my real self. I felt liked, enjoyed, and maybe even admired, but without being authentic with family, friends, and all humanity, I couldn't truly and fully be loved. As my love of running and triathlons became a passionate force in my life, I learned that I also raced better when I was *more* present. I applied this to my work, my relationships, and my overall existence, and I allowed moments of living in my passion to teach me. I had to be me if I was to love and be loved. I am not a victim. I am not an imposter. I desire to be fully and wholly present.

Once I became more present in myself, my eyes could open to more lessons.

This awareness did not "fix" anything, but as I started doing a lot of thinking, soul-searching, and emotional work to continue to learn and evolve, I became more content and also more curious. I embraced my roles and truly strived to see, hear, and understand people in my roles of wife, mother, coach, friend, daughter, sister, and whoever else I'm called to be. I opened my eyes to the truth that when living a life in which I am more connected to the good and bad of my human experience, *I know how and why I got here.* I got here by navigating most of my young life with blind confidence, youthful belief and faith, the overwhelming grace and support of my family, a lot of fun, and quite a few missteps. In the fall of 2017, I started to be able to look at the present and reflect on the past to see that I got here by living a disconnected human existence.

After understanding the root and evolution of my progress, I still remained hesitant to write my story. I grew up wanting to be a writer and believing I would someday be one. I knew I had something to say and believed that endurance athletes and any human who wants a real life full of passion and awareness can benefit from my work, but my viewpoint was clouded by some old default ways of thinking. When feeling the urge to share myself, I suddenly felt raw and exposed. I didn't like losing the certainty I felt with control. I celebrated the lessons in the works of my greatest mentors: Brené Brown, Brooke Castillo of the Life Coach School, Glennon Doyle, and many more inspiring female writers. I yearned to *be* these women, to have had a major "aha moment" that catapulted me into the place of "knowing." I waited for the courage and wanted the degrees, the experience, and the following, in order to make my voice bigger and louder. I wanted to effect change. But part of me still wanted to fall back into unawareness.

I sought to control and justify my expertise by seeking out validation from those I believed would give it to me rather than challenge me. I considered going back to school or trying to get a job working under any of the mentors I admired. Often, listening to and believing my fear-driven thoughts led me to consider giving up on all of it and putting all my energy into shrinking myself to be content being quieter and "smaller." I believed I could instead find comfort in returning to the safety of being disconnected from myself. For the longest time, while living a successful professional existence, I allowed this fear and self-doubt to still hold me back. By doing so, I was missing the biggest message that all my mentors were reminding me of: I have everything I need right now in me. I am still worthy.

The life I desire is to be a coach and mentor who gives more than a solid training and nutrition plan. I want to teach people how to use endurance sports to learn more about the power of embracing the full human experience. In turn, I want this to also benefit their athletic performance and overall existence. I want to support systems and ideas that help people return to deep self-discovery. I want people to be filled up from within so we can work together to serve humanity better and create meaningful change. I want to educate others on the value of self-perception. I want to write—to inspire through action and experience. This book is the story of my ever-continuing transformation through endurance sports and my relationships. These are the lessons I have learned from coaching, training, and racing and the inspiration of many amazing friends, family, coaches, authors, and mentors.

I am far better aware of myself for going further. And my hope is that you will find the passion to propel yourself toward self-discovery so that you can dare mighty and embrace the fullness of the human experience.

I KNOW I BELONG

I grew up and live in Wisconsin. As a lifelong midwesterner, I am accustomed to daily shifting weather patterns. But when temperatures get closer to forty degrees Fahrenheit, and you add wind and a cold drizzle, I find them to be some of the most intolerable weather conditions of all. So, when I woke up with the intention of running before work on a dreary September morning in 2019, I decided to hop on the treadmill and watch Netflix rather than hit the road. I tried to turn the treadmill on, and it did nothing. I went through my very limited "fix-it" plans; I turned it on and off, unplugged it and plugged it back in, and pretended to check the circuit breaker before realizing I had to run outside or not at all.

I love to listen to audiobooks or podcasts while running. Although I am a voracious reader—and never on a device, but actual books—I love to listen to personal improvement books while pounding out many miles. On that dreary, cold, windy, dark, rainy day, I felt like Glennon Doyle was reading her bestselling book, *Untamed*, to *me*. After almost five miles, I returned home with a strong passion and vigor to write from my heart. I also returned with an even more powerful desire to get to know myself better. This led me to capture a written glimpse of who I am now, and I hope my vulnerability will inspire you to do the same.

WHO I AM AND WILL BECOME

I am a human woman who cares deeply for all humanity.
I am imperfect, but I believe now that I am not and never have
    been broken.
I have many flaws but am continually committed to practicing
    accepting and growing from them.
I have failed often.
I passionately believe I have always been exactly where I
    needed to be at the moment.
I will no longer allow myself to be frustrated for not knowing,
    because part of my journey has always been and will con-
    tinue to be to gain wisdom along the way.
I trust myself and understand the importance of letting go of
    all relationships that don't honor my values and support
    me. I trust others who trust themselves.
I am ready to feel *all* of life and accept that there will be hurt,
    discomfort, and pain. I don't want to miss one second of
    my life. I am learning to love more and better, without fear,
    rigidity, or judgment.

I desire to love and be loved deeply. I seek people who surround me with honesty, love, and grace.

I believe in boundaries.

I am a leader. I consider myself an expert coach, but I will always keep learning.

I love my husband so much that it often scares the controlling part of me, and I believe he is the man I am meant to be with right now in my life.

I love my children in ways that words cannot convey and am excited to continue to know them throughout their lives.

I love my parents and mother-in-law and feel extremely grateful for the lessons they have modeled and taught me.

I love my brothers and their families and feel a yearning when I go long periods without enveloping my nieces and nephews in giant hugs.

I love God and my connection to him and my faith through worship, Bible studies, and prayer.

I love music and dancing. I live to be outdoors, and I love to watch and play sports.

I love good sex.

I love the ritual of drinking morning coffee so much that as soon as I drink the last drop, I look forward to waking up in the morning to have another cup.

Out of choice, I go to bed early and wake up before sunrise.

Traveling makes me feel alive, and I hope to see most of the world before I die.

I love sunshine and the joy it always brings.

I enjoy biking and swimming, but I *love* running.

I am privileged to be able to dream and have the confidence to achieve my goals.

I love to laugh and enjoy moments when life feels easy and light.

I am an extrovert who loves to be with people and friends. But as an empath, the daily maintenance of relationships can often overwhelm me.

I love a wild party as much as curling up with a great book.

I hate my phone and texting, although I respect it as an important communication tool in this era of technology.

I understand my purpose in this one crazy life. I am a coach who is meant to lead others to actualizing their goals.

I am a writer and believe my words and experiences are worthy of being shared with others.

I am a woman who is here to be an example of living with love, acceptance, and peace with oneself, inspiring others to do the same.

I live to be an inspiration that anything is possible. I am thankful that I have found this through my passion for health, fitness, and racing, which I share with so many.

I will share and challenge people and ideas while also learning to be less rigid and "right."

I will continue to practice being more understanding and compassionate.

I will not question my voice or judge the amount of impact I need to have in the world for it to matter.

I will continue to see and challenge my own comfort.

I will proudly work for what I believe in. I am here to learn and grow while also being the real me.

HOW YOU CAN LEARN FROM ME

- Build a foundation of self-awareness. Self-awareness is vital to mental and emotional well-being. This allows for more meaningful relationships, clearer decision-making and more exciting goal setting, connecting more to yourself in present moments, and identifying and following your passions. Start with the simple activity of writing your own "Who I Am and Will Become" statement in order to reflect on how well you know yourself.
- Be open to constant personal evolution. Understand that you are always changing. Stay curious about yourself and your purpose in life.
- Keep learning. When you are open to continual self-discovery, you can apply this knowledge while learning more with each opportunity. Being aware and mindful allows for true *life-changing* experiences. This connection to yourself will help you live with less fear and fully actualize your potential.
- Know yourself first so that you can attack goals fully. Establish this self-awareness and understanding to identify how your vision of yourself affects your processes and outcomes. Use this information to increase your athletic prowess.

PART 1

FOUNDATIONAL LESSONS

The courage to be vulnerable is not about winning or losing, it's about the courage to show up when you can't predict or control the outcome.
BRENÉ BROWN, *DARING GREATLY*

STAY CURIOUS

MY FIRST EXPOSURE TO THE IRONMAN TRIATHLON was a relatively uneventful, brief conversation with a new friend. We moved into our first home in Madison, Wisconsin, in the summer of 2004, and later that year I met my across-the-street neighbor, Christine. Christine and I shared our Christian faith and stories of motherhood. In these conversations, she also told me that she had raced sprint distance triathlons in Florida as a sponsored triathlete and was an Ironman finisher. That day she said, humbly yet somewhat flippantly, "It is only exercising for seventeen hours; anyone can do it." She also told me about her friend Amanda, who had a group of friends, a triathlon club of sorts, called Amanda's Play Group (APG). When I left her house that day, I reflected on how much I liked Christine, but I was mostly unaffected by her comments and enthusiasm for the sport of triathlon. I realize now, however, that she likely ignited a curious spark in me.

Sometime later, when I saw the 2005 Gatorade commercial featuring Chris Legh collapsing fifty meters from the finish line at the 1997 Ironman World Championships in Kona, Hawaii, I was even more curious. The Ironman event had been happening once a year in Madison since 2002 and all over the world since 1978. This commercial highlighted a gaunt, dehydrated man approaching the finish line with all the ease and grace of a newborn colt. Even though the commercial itself was unglamorous, something about this event triggered a desire in me. I started asking more locals about the race and ended up meeting many people who raced triathlons, and even some more—other than Christine—who had competed in this crazy Ironman event.

My curiosity led me to load up the kids to watch the bike portion of Ironman Wisconsin that September. Wearing a large poncho, I watched in awe as athletes zoomed by, seemingly unaffected by the nonstop pouring rain. Spectators cheered as if it were the Olympics. I went home, and, after putting the kids to bed, I tuned into the live coverage online for hours, watching age-group athletes cross the finish line after an entire day of racing. They were soaking wet and exhausted, but they had giant smiles of accomplishment and elation. I cried tears of joy for people I had never met, wearing their garbage-bag ponchos and dragging their soggy feet to complete such a challenging goal. From that moment, I was hooked. I set out with the intention of someday competing in Ironman Wisconsin.

The next day—yes, I am and always have been impulsive—I told Jamie about my new life goal to take on the 2.4-mile swim, 112-mile bike ride, and 26.2-mile run. He has always been an amazingly supportive husband, and, although neither of us had any idea what this would entail, he encouraged me to go for it. At this time I could only swim enough to save my life, run a couple of miles at a time, and ride on my hybrid bike with the kids in tow. But I was able to tap into some of my youthful confidence. I trusted myself to believe that if I put my mind to this goal, I could be resourceful enough to achieve it. And Jamie believed it as well.

After making the decision, I was lucky enough to have an immediate strong mentor in Christine. I sought her out and excitedly told her my revelation, but I also admitted I didn't know how to lap swim or have any idea what kind of bike to buy. She happened to be a swim instructor and encouraged me to sign up for a "masters" swim class. To say I hated going to this swim class would be an understatement. Looking back, I know this hatred was due to the fact I really didn't like doing things that would expose my flaws. And not being a natural-born swimmer, I was as far from a "master" as I could be.

Christine was kind, patient, and matter-of-fact with me during each class. I would fix one element of my stroke while at the same time feeling like I was undoing everything else I'd learned. Even though I had grown up as an athlete (ball sports), had solid core strength, and felt like I had a strong mind-body connection, I struggled to nail down an efficient swim form and technique.

Learning to swim is still one of my biggest life lessons in the power of persevering with curiosity.

I would get up most mornings and literally cry thinking of going to the swim class to be critiqued and criticized. I wanted to blame Christine for her blunt approach, but I also felt dependent on her for my success.

I didn't like the loss of control, but I still showed up twice a week, eventually adding a solo session weekly as well. And eventually through hard work, humility, and consistency, I learned how to swim. And then I even moved into a faster lane. My stroke wasn't perfect, but I got stronger, faster, and more confident. Later, when I finished my first half-iron swim in Iowa on that day in 2008, I was drunk on the giddiness that comes with accomplishing something that was extremely difficult. I am very thankful for Christine's guidance, expertise, and encouragement. I am also thankful for her humble message of "anyone can do it" (Ironman). This message has stuck with me, and I have used it to encourage so many people to race over many years as both an athlete and coach.

I joined Amanda's Play Group (APG) as well. The core group of mostly men and only a handful of women were older than me, and most of them were experienced triathletes and Ironman finishers. They taught me without judgment, helped me train hard, and made sure I knew what to expect going into my races in the years leading up to Ironman Wisconsin 2009. This group showed me that if you are curious, confident enough to try, yet humble enough to learn, you will have great success. Amanda, my first coach, guided me with an excellent balance of fun, education, and work to prepare me for my goal of finishing the race. Ironman 2009 was an amazing day with so much support from my wonderful family, many friends, and fellow members of APG. It is true that you will always remember your first.

HOW YOU CAN LEARN FROM ME

- Stay curious. To believe that anything is possible, you have to understand the importance of being curious. Try new things. Show up with a humble willingness to learn.

- Know that you are worthy and valuable. When someone compliments or encourages you to take a leap, consider why they are saying it. Don't talk yourself out of big things. Anything is possible.
- Don't focus too much on what you don't know. Submerge yourself in the process and stay present in it each day. Let it unfold, but also seek out mentors who can answer questions and gently come alongside you for your learning process.

BE HONEST WITH YOURSELF FIRST

As I mentioned, in 2017, I signed up to compete in my third Ironman Wisconsin race alongside my husband, friends, and Zone Racing athletes. Why? I knew that all the people I primarily spent my time with would be consumed by training. I would be involved through my work anyway. And I would always have long-ride training partners. All these reasons were true, and the training experience was extremely memorable and overwhelmingly positive. But I always felt, in the depths of me, that a tiny morsel of something was missing.

In September of that year, I finished the race just a few minutes after my husband, Jamie, with an Ironman distance personal record (PR) as well as a one-hour run PR. I was satisfied, pleasantly exhausted, and excited for Jamie, the athletes I had coached, and my teammates and friends. I proudly cheered as they crossed the finish line, one by one, with elated smiles and in awe of accomplishing their first Ironman finish. Five of the eleven of our finishers were female friends who had become long-ride training partners, and this event was my first time experiencing the Ironman triathlon journey with a group of women. My heart burst with joy for them, bringing forth tears of happiness. At the finish line, we hugged and celebrated, but I still had this nagging feeling there was a tiny hole in my heart. And although I never wavered in my amazement of their achievements, the hole allowed my joy for my personal accomplishment to slowly leak out. In the days immediately following the race, I chalked up these feelings to my narcissistic tendencies or the fact I was always in the position of authority, so it was my job to be happier for others rather than for myself. I justified it all by reminding myself that I had set out to race *for* them, even though they didn't ask me to or want me to. I decided that should be good enough. And it was good, but I still felt the urge to examine these feelings further.

So I read books, blogs, and articles on various self-discovery topics. I listened to podcasts and self-reflected. I sought out answers. I eventually came to the realization I was falling into a comfort zone of caring for others—not only because I genuinely love to motivate and encourage people but also because I was using my job to avoid being personally vulnerable to many experiences and relationships in my life, and this included new goals. And although I had been *working* on self-care and growth, I was not being fully honest with myself. I still hadn't learned that the path I would most benefit from would not "fix me," but return me to a place of fully *knowing myself.* This lack of feeling fully present at the time blocked my ability to feel a full sense of belonging.

I wanted to honestly know myself better, to understand my purpose, and to be sure that I honored it in life and in each goal along the way.

Building a solid foundation of physical, emotional, and mental health relies deeply on knowing yourself and believing you inherently belong. This *knowing* allows for an honest relationship with yourself, which is key to having honest relationships with others. In order to create and maintain a healthy lifestyle, it is vital to know and care for yourself well. Often when I say these things, people assume I want them to *define* their life roles and *pamper* themselves. This kind of self-care is especially marketed heavily to women. And although these messages are not always negative, they are not what I recommend for reaching overall wellness.

- *To know yourself* is to understand your strengths and weaknesses, passions and fears, desires and dreams. It means being aware of your likes, dislikes, quirks, tolerances, and limitations. Knowing yourself means staying curious about your purpose as you continually evolve through life. To understand your humanness.
- *To care for yourself* is to put your needs first so that you are better able to serve others. True belonging is not only taking up the same space or enjoying the same hobbies as other people. Belonging happens when you know yourself and show up as you. If you know yourself, you will always know you belong to you. Put basically: you need to stay curious and open in order to have the most fulfilling life and overall wellness.

When you know yourself, you can show up to your goals and surround yourself with honest, supportive relationships.

On the September Ironman day in 2017, and the months leading up to it, I understood the importance of always being honest and had identified it as a top value in relationships. I was willing to invest in the people I was coaching, and that often meant saying hard things to help them grow. But throughout that process, I didn't show up *honestly* as me. I didn't fully insert myself into the role of supportive coach and training partner who was racing only for others. On the flip side, I also didn't fully commit to reaching my capabilities as an athlete. Instead, I straddled two goals, or two "whys." I have no regrets, as it was still one of the best years and experiences of my life. I am extremely thankful for the lessons I learned from the experience and the athletes with whom I took the journey. And these lessons and relationships continue to teach me. Although I am far from perfect, I now have a more open and honest relationship with myself. I approach life with a more thoughtful, vulnerable attitude. I consider how my goals fit into my overarching why and my specific purpose for each smaller goal along the way. I funnel most of my decisions through that view and am a better wife, mom, friend, daughter, sister, coach, and athlete because of it. And more than anything, I am willing to examine my flaws without (as much) judgment. I can make mistakes and learn from them.

You must be honest with yourself to believe in your worth and understand your purpose.

When we are born, we don't question our worth. As a baby, I would cry and scream whenever I had a need or want. I instinctively knew I was worthy of care, and that was corroborated when someone came to my rescue whenever I had a dirty diaper or was hungry. As I grew up, my well-intentioned parents did what all parents do—reward good behavior and punish bad. I slowly started to believe the message that our worthiness is earned by what we do. I now see I was blessed to grow up in a house that didn't often or intentionally reinforce the idea of unworthiness. I was allowed to make mistakes and was still loved and accepted by my mom. And I didn't grow up in the current climate, where the accepted standard dictates that kids should only take on activities that they are already *good at*. As I entered adolescence and adulthood, however, society began to chip into my inherent sense of value by reminding me that the scale of worthiness is based on appearances, actions, and roles rather than a birthright.

As a young woman, I also believed that women's worth is directly connected to how we look. As this misinformation began to trickle into my mind and soul, I learned how to *manage my persona and appearance* to prove my worth rather than *honestly know and believe* it.

This seeped into all my relationships and interactions, eventually clouding my understanding of my personal values.

The mental and emotional experience of my Ironman 2017 training triggered something deep within me. I started to figure out how my lack of belief in my personal value had contributed to my not going "all in" on my goal. After winning an award in my first triathlon (more on that later), I established my worth in being a faster than average female cyclist. I believed I would maintain my worth as a coach and athlete if I kept being *fast*. This pressure derailed me often, sometimes in training when I was instructed to slow down, but I didn't want to feel bad about my pace or post a slow time on the social media training app, Strava. When I raced, I would get wrapped up in comparisons and results. If I wasn't going to be *fast*, I began preparing my excuses. Years after becoming a coach, I often believed I had to work hard to prove myself rather than be receptive to the idea that I had to fail in order to learn the lessons that would help me improve. I spent time hyperfocused on what I didn't know rather than understanding and believing in the value of being a lifelong learner. I made all things my personal conquests instead of believing the best thing I could do was to return to myself. I fell into a lack of outward confidence in my abilities and considered changing careers. I was detached and afraid, and it permeated my entire life.

I realized in 2018 that something had to change in how I defined my worthiness and honestly put myself out into the world. As an athlete, I believed for many years that I needed to earn and validate my worth by being fast, going farther, having years of race experience, owning the best gear, or winning awards. My insecurities and fears taught me that I must flash my "worthiness credentials" in order to compete. Thankfully, albeit cracked and hidden under many layers of lies, my young foundation of innate worthiness remained, allowing me to believe that although I might not win, I could still show up. This foundation hadn't been maintained for a long time, so it was weak. But *I had something to build on*. Rather than having to focus on building my worth, I could spend my time rebuilding it through *training*, a very familiar concept. I was able to rebuild my notion of self-worth through the practice of *daily*, *realistic* positive affirmations—often in the form of reading Bible verses, journaling, and prayer. I focused on my competencies and nourished them by doing the things I was good at and not minimizing them to make others more comfortable. I then had to be more comfortable accepting compliments while examining my inner critic with curiosity while practicing self-grace and compassion. I started to be more honest and return to *myself*.

In addition to revamping my training, I also went to therapy to help me recover my self-worth. My therapist helped me explore my need for outward validation and told me that I was too hard on myself. She reminded me that I had all I needed within me to be a worthy woman, wife, mother, friend, daughter, sister, athlete, trainer, and coach. I was worthy enough to love and be loved, and I didn't need to prove myself to anyone. I was and am enough. Then I trained my mind and my heart. I practiced. I sought opportunities to learn lessons through my passion for racing. I still learn and practice, and I am sharing my lessons with more confidence, knowing I am worthy of doing so.

In the fall of 2018, I had the amazing opportunity to put my heart and mind into a new race process for the Ironman Arizona 70.3 with some of my best friends. In the months leading up to the race, I challenged my body not only through swimming, cycling, and running but also with indoor heat acclimation sessions, training in sweat suits, and enduring long sauna visits. I set out with an intention of showing up fully as an athlete. I applied the lessons I was learning about myself to my mental preparation. For the trip to Arizona, I packed my nutrition and followed my race plan exactly as written. I went to bed early and practiced visualization, knowing my why and believing I was worthy of giving my all. I was there to be present within myself, even if the outcome was still uncertain. I arrived at a race site I had never been to before, confident I would do my best—but there was nothing to "earn" or "prove." I had made the choice that this is what I wanted to do, and I was there to follow through with this goal, this promise to myself. It was still hard, and I was humbled in many ways. But I believe I showed up honestly to my experience. I raced as the worthy athlete that I am.

HOW YOU CAN LEARN FROM ME

- Be honest. With yourself and with others.
- Focus on truth with love in order to reach your goals. Be honestly vulnerable with yourself. Practice self-compassion alongside honesty.
- Know your worthiness. Practice the belief that you were born with all the worth you need in you. Stay curious about your needs and wants, and educate yourself on what could potentially be influencing you from the outside. Honor them so that you can best serve others.
- Surround yourself with people who support honesty.

- Leave nothing to chance or open for excuses when going after big goals.

BE WHOLLY YOU

Through much of my journey, I saw myself as someone who needed to be fixed, and for a long time I thought that striving would be the answer to arriving at feeling content and peaceful. I see the flaw in this way of thinking now, and thankfully I no longer see myself as "broken," nor do I seek out growth from a place of panic or urgency. I am more aware and present, staying curious about myself and all aspects of my life. This has allowed me to live even more in the both/and space, learning that I can even have thoughts, values, and belief systems that society says contradict or oppose each other. I feel I can give my full, real self to the world.

In my younger years, I equated being a feminist with hating men. I see clearly now that this way of thinking was a product of ignorance, societal influence, and some cultural conditioning. I thought that if I celebrated being a woman, demanding change and equality, then it would be from a place of bringing men *down* to our level instead of lifting all of us *up*. Through years of learning, and ultimately seeing the world differently, I now support the truth of feminist thinking; after all, the definition of *feminism*, according to *Merriam-Webster,* is "belief in and advocacy of the political, economic, and social equality of the sexes expressed especially through organized activity on behalf of women's rights and interests." How could I not be a feminist? I had been defining characteristics of women and female relationships through a negative and untrusting lens, based on earlier experiences that did not model healthy and robust female friendships. When I eventually learned to be more vulnerable to trusting women, I wanted to work more and more to lift all of us up. This naturally led to making this a part of my purpose in life.

I am here to educate and encourage every woman to live as her authentic self.

As a white female in the United States, I grew up mostly naive to the societal hurdles in place solely because of my gender. My social conditioning created several blind spots personally, but I could more easily see the obstacles affecting many of my personal training clients and athletes. And as I saw more examples of inequity, it became clear how the ripples of cultural conditioning also affected my daughter, friends, and family.

I was fortunate to be able to take a solo work trip to Colorado for the TrainingPeaks Coaching Conference in 2019. In addition to this opening my eyes to a clearer understanding of my professional worth and leveling up my confidence in my coaching capabilities, my purpose in endurance sports took on another facet. As a coach, I have been in the presence of many men who have shown their real selves to me. While no one is totally immune to cultural conditioning around gender, I believe I have provided a safe space where they can be fully seen and heard. I have truly *listened* to men's raw hurt, fear, and disappointment without judgment, and I have seen their tears. I have helped guide them through goal setting and reaching those goals in a way that honors themselves rather than society's definition of *masculinity*. And it has been and continues to be an honor to be in a trusting relationship with so many. I get to be a front-seat witness as the sport of triathlon adds value to their entire lives rather than breeding a stereotypical narcissistic, macho approach and viewpoint.

When I attended the conference in 2019, I had been using triathlon for years as a tool for teaching people the importance of knowing and caring for themselves, but it was there I learned more about the importance and different needs for guiding and teaching *women*. As a personal trainer, group exercise instructor, and coach, I had always been extremely interested in the psychology behind fitness. I love to listen and ask questions, to get to know people at a deeper level, to see them and understand what drives their choices. And while I enjoy working hard with and for my male clients and athletes, I have also felt a sense of ease, connection, and care for women. And in perfect timing, this conference was highlighting women in the sport. It was where I was introduced to the groundbreaking research of Dr. Stacy Sims and the women of Live Feisty Media. I soaked in the new information on how to train women with respect to our unique physiology from Dr. Sims (I recommend her book *Roar*) and typed pages of notes on how I could implement her methods for my clients. I was also drawn toward the work of Sara Gross of Live Feisty. I strongly desired to continue learning from the mission of her company. Not only did I want to give people the tools and encouragement to become stronger athletes and humans; I also realized I needed to be a part of their movement to influence the culture.

I returned home on fire with new ideas and excited to create a new coaching platform for my athletes. I felt different. Over the weekend I had realized what was already true: I am an expert in what I do and have a clear and defined purpose for it. I also knew what I hadn't known before, which was that I desired a bigger platform if I was to reach more than one person at a time and incite cultural change. And I believed I could. I started small, including more mental and emotional training in my established athletes. I wrote a curriculum that focused on using racing to add value to an individual's life and then in turn help them become a stronger athlete. I focused on encouraging more women to try the sport, regardless of experience, knowledge, abilities, or gear. I mentored them and encouraged them to join our racing team. Kelly and I met with local members of the community and created plans for our team to serve and give back through volunteering and raising awareness of bike safety. We decided to host a free youth clinic to help prepare all kids for the large annual Oregon Kids Triathlon. We were gaining momentum as a team, and I was growing professionally. And then COVID-19 hit.

As a highly extroverted person with three highly extroverted teens at home, I had my own challenges during the restrictions. And although Jamie had mostly asymptomatic COVID-19 at one point, we were otherwise blessed with good health. It was still hard. As restaurant owners, it was scary, because Jaime's lifework, also our main source of income and our livelihood, was threatened. The division and uncertainty were exhausting and damaging. I missed people. I craved hugs. But it was also good. We had space and time to get to know our teens again at a point when we had been all going in different directions. The pace of life slowed, allowing for time to think and for me to consider what I really wanted and needed personally and professionally. I learned from watching people overcome adversity daily, sometimes minute to minute. And I had time to work on a project I had been slowly tinkering with since being inspired in the fall of 2018 at the conference in Boulder. I had the mental space to do what I always dreamed of doing—write this book.

I also worked with my fifteen-year-old son, Quinton, to grow my Instagram following. I got excited to share content I felt would not glorify me but add value to the world. And after much encouragement and support from my husband, family, and so many amazing friends, I launched my blog on our website. My blog reaches many people with messages of self-awareness, compassion, and care. It aims to teach, inspire, and lead others to live their authentic lives so that we can better humanity. I love to write that weekly blog. And although races were constantly getting canceled, I kept training. I realized how much I rely on my daily exercise routine to calm my mind, ease my anxiety, and stabilize me to be able to meet the challenges of my day. And I love when my daily training has a purpose and a goal.

I also used my energy to give back to my longtime Zone community, first offering free online cycling sessions during lockdown, using them to raise money for a short-term charitable cause that my husband delivered through his businesses to feed families in need during the financial crunch. I started writing for TrainingPeaks, Live Feisty Media, and *Triathlete Magazine* online. I listened to all the Feisty podcasts and followed everyone and everything they did. And when they hosted an online three-day Feisty Women's Performance Summit, I signed up and offered to lead a virtual ride for attendees. And after first being told they had someone else, when that person fell through at the last minute, I took the opportunity and had a fun ride. I also joined the Feisty Triathlon team and ordered swag to represent the company and their cause. I believed I belonged there.

In April 2021, after the performance summit, I reached out to Karen at Feisty with a podcast idea. She passed the idea onto Sara Gross, and Sara reached out about the podcast, but also with a potential to contract as a coach for the Feisty Triathlon Team and brand. I had enormous respect for Sara as an athlete and trailblazing woman. She is a thought leader in the sport of triathlon and for equality for women and minorities, with the overall goal to shift the culture for women in sport. My dream of being involved in the Live Feisty mission and brand was officially realized when I was made Feisty Triathlon head coach and lead educator and invited to speak at their Level Up Summit, a virtual event in May 2021. I was gifted the amazing opportunity, in part due to my abilities and boldness, and the time working on a team with Karen, Jasmine, and Emily added immense value to my life.

Although I no longer am employed with Feisty, I am beyond thankful for the opportunities I had during my time there. I completed Dr. Sims's Women Are Not Small Men and Menopause for Athletes courses, and the knowledge I gained has been invaluable to my coaching and personal racing career. My eyes were opened further to the impact and influence that our culture has on us. And I gained more knowledge on how to coach men and women differently from a physiological standpoint, in addition to acknowledging the different mental and societal challenges each face. I am able to encourage them to be wholly themselves.

I believe I was and am meant to participate in endurance sports. It has honestly made me a better mom, wife, and coach. I very much enjoy the three triathlon sports and practicing the art of putting them all together. I love the physical, mental, and emotional challenges that present themselves and the satisfaction of overcoming them, either in success or failure. I thrive on the camaraderie and in the community. I also experience the truth that women often have a hard time considering their own needs and wants ahead of others. We are taught that being called "selfless" is the highest compliment we can receive, a word that *Merriam-Webster* defines as "having no concern for self." How can women train and race an endurance event that requires months of preparation if we have no time or concern for ourselves?

I believe we can be focused on our own needs or desires AND have concern for others.

We heap expectations on ourselves, some due to cultural conditioning and some from the pressures of partners or competition from other women (also a product of our culture). We are often saddled with this idea of "mom guilt" if we have children and take *any* amount of time to build ourselves up (more on this later). Although men face their own societal pressures, they do not include the requirement that they spend every available moment in the presence of their children. I have never heard a man say he is suffering from "dad guilt."

According to a 2018 study, "Gender Inequality in Household Chores and Work-Family Conflict," women assume markedly more of the household tasks than men—specifically, caring for children (thirty-eight hours a week for women versus twenty-three for men), caring for family members (twenty hours for women versus fourteen for men), and household chores (twenty hours for women versus eleven for men). So, although women now form a large part of the labor force, they still do the majority of domestic work. This work takes a lot of time and energy, so not only do women lack time to have big personal goals, but they also are often too physically, emotionally, and mentally exhausted to have the bandwidth to even consider their own wants and needs.

I want to be very clear: I am not suggesting that all women must choose to work or have hobbies away from home. Telling women what they *should* do is the exact opposite of my message. I am also not naive enough to think it is simple for all women to implement a plan to realize their dreams, especially not quickly. Regardless of gender, it is always important to practice unselfish behavior often, putting the needs of others over your own. But I have personally learned that doing so is more rewarding and loving when it comes from a place of wholly believing in yourself.

I certainly became a better coach, a better athlete, and a stronger woman overall when I began to think outside the culture's defined roles and my own conditioning. It has afforded me the ability to see others more fully and offer inspiration and guidance to my athletes to do the same. In my younger life, I chose to take on more unpaid work and care for the home and/or kids, but when I became interested in the triathlon, I chose to prioritize my career and hobby of racing as well. And although it looks a little different these days, I still prioritize relationships, and I hope I always will. Since living as the most authentic version of me—the person I was created to be—I have been more able to care for others and give back to my community without resentment and bitterness. I have more personal respect and compassion. Is this selfish? No. Does it help me and my loved ones? And does it allow me to serve humanity better? Yes.

I have worked hard to cultivate trust within my circles of women friends and colleagues. I was confident enough to seek out mentors and other strong women pushing not only for individual understanding but also for big cultural change. As more research surfaces around female athletics, I am able to seek it out and apply it to my own training and for my female clients. We no longer need to train as "small men" (a popular Dr. Sim's phrase) but can implement some new strategies for female-specific training. There is no more hiding the fact that bleeding monthly is healthy and normal for premenopausal women. And no more fear about bodily and mental changes through the seasons of life. We are and continue to be empowered to learn about these changes and to change the narrative for future generations. Girls can aspire to compete through all stages of life. Women can be empowered to embrace their changing bodies rather than decide they are now "too old" to do the hobbies they love or to try new ones.

HOW YOU CAN LEARN FROM ME

- Be wholly you. Be a good student of yourself. You are the only person you spend every single second of your life with. Be open to lifelong learning and to thinking and feeling differently at any time of your life.

- Know that you are unique. Celebrate your individuality. Learn more about your own physiology and how it can impact sport. Try new things.
- Humbly seek out mentorship. Forge connections with those who have more information or are further along on a similar path.
- Communicate your dreams. We all fall victim to outside influence. When you see it impacting you, try to make changes to return to yourself.

LIVE WITH PASSION

In 2008, I ran the Madison Half Marathon with two girlfriends. There was nothing notable from a racing standpoint about this race—no big "aha" moments, or a PR. The race itself doesn't really stand out in my memory at all, but it is still a special race to me. I covered the 13.1 miles with Kylie, a friend who had positively influenced my view on life then and in ways that still continue to unfold today. My friend Ella and I encouraged her along the way, and after running stride by stride we all crossed the finish line together. She was tired and excited, and I was joyfully content with my opportunity to have given back to a friend who had given me so much, a friend who helped ignite and nurture my ability to dream and live with passion.

I had met Kylie four years earlier. At twenty-three, recovering from the birth of my second child and first son, I was disappointed with my physical appearance. I felt puffy and noticed that my butt had drooped to become part of my legs. I loved being a mom, and I was also grossly unhappy with my flat bottom, leaky and larger-than-life boobs, and an overall flabby physique. Jamie supported my desire to "get my body back" by supporting a yearlong membership at the local fitness club. This small choice, albeit a bit misguided and harsh on myself, was impactful in ways I could not have anticipated, far beyond my physical appearance.

So, in January 2004, I joined the throng of excited, well-intentioned new gym-goers. My kids liked to wake up at 5:00 a.m., and so each day we were fully ready to be the first people at the door of the free gym childcare center. The Kids' Club facility was state of the art and boasted a huge indoor jungle gym. The women who worked in the playroom loved to engage with the kids, whether it was holding and rocking the baby or entertaining my one-year-old with themed craft projects. I got into a routine of running on the treadmill or using the elliptical machine and eventually joined strength-based classes. I found myself not only starting to enjoy the person I was becoming physically but also the fact I was blooming into connecting to myself deeper than I ever had. This is when I met my friend Kylie.

Kylie was truly one of the most influential women in my young adult life. Her strength, intelligence, and healthy "I don't give a fuck" attitude was magnetic at a time when I was (unknowingly) searching for a guiding mentor. Kylie's young daughters also frequented the Kids' Club, and at first we would unintentionally choose treadmills next to each other. I didn't know I needed an open friend who would inspire me to begin to develop the honesty, confidence, and wisdom needed to live my most authentic life.

Over time our Monday runs became a staple in my week. Our warm-up included exchanging fun weekend stories and catching up on small talk. As we ran, as our bodies heated up and we got into a physical groove, our conversations went from surface level to deep confessions filled with heartfelt honesty about all of life. Kylie shared many of her life's failures and how she learned from and continued to learn from them. Her example showed me that *it's okay to make mistakes and own them honestly.* She also taught me about the vital importance of taking care of yourself in order to be able to fully serve others. Kylie exuded a quiet passion for self-compassion that was foreign to me. Her bold storytelling helped me consider how to start to let go of reacting to emotions such as worry, insecurity, shame, and guilt. She modeled a life of less hustle and was more engaged in her surroundings. Her vulnerability taught me about trust and grace. She encouraged me to remain curious and wholly present.

My mom loved us greatly and showed us by forgoing her own personal dreams and desires after having me when she was eighteen years old. My dad supported her in this role, working his ass off to provide for us. Although I know now this was an intentional decision they had made as partners, I did not know that while growing up. Until meeting Kylie, I had never considered the impact that the relationship and roles that my parents modeled, combined with overarching cultural definitions, had on my way of defining parenting roles. Jamie encouraged me as a partner, and I was and am an equal participant in how we defined our roles and duties at home and with the kids. I was doing what I wanted to do to take care of my own needs, yet I would still suffer from guilt. Whenever I told Kylie I felt guilty about leaving my kids in the playroom for two hours so I could workout, chat with friends, and take a long shower, she would encourage me to inspect my feelings of guilt. Were they showing me something I needed to change or alter? Were these feelings leading me back to more understanding? I realized my own upbringing and years of cultural influences were leading me to think that if I did something to nurture my own passions I needed to also feel guilt. Kylie reminded me that I could have these feelings while still fully enjoying my workout. Her mindset and lesson to me was that we often think consistent guilt is productive, but recognizing guilt is more of a chance to reflect on our decisions.

Doing something we enjoy while cultivating, focusing on, and reacting to guilt at the same time only negates the joy.

This still resonates strongly with me fourteen years later. When I feel guilty, I remain curious and inspect the feeling. I decide if I need to take the time to deeply reflect and/or change something. Sometimes I need to acknowledge and allow the feeling while not reacting. I have used this practice over all my emotions. I wish I could report I have perfected it, but instead I have identified it as another thing I will continue to practice.

Kylie was and is a runner, effortlessly banging out seven miles on the treadmill when I met her. But Kylie did not believe she should be defined as either a runner or an athlete. In addition to the wisdom Kylie shared through her experiences, I also learned that *strong women have fears and insecurities—and that doesn't make them weak.* In fact, now I know how much more courage it takes to admit to and discuss life's uncertainties. I also learned that *all women, even the strongest feminists, are affected by the messaging of our culture.* At the half-marathon finish line, I asked if she believed then that she could add "runner" to her list of roles, and she just laughed. Although Kylie was incredibly self-aware, she could not fully outrun the impact of how our culture defines athletes. I am beyond thankful for Kylie's honesty and our mutual encouragement to passionately dream alongside our roles as moms and wives. Our friendship never extended too far beyond running—and only off the treadmills occasionally in our training for the half-marathon—but it did leave a lasting impression on my heart and soul.

Ironically, frequent use of the treadmill taught me lessons as well. As an inanimate object, the lessons were obviously not as heartfelt as my conversations with Kylie. But as I gained fitness and started making new goals, I was thankful for the treadmill, even if it meant hours on end running nowhere while the sun was shining outside. It was a wonderful tool that gave me the ability to train for big goals throughout my third pregnancy and beyond as I continued to take the kids to the gym playroom. I still teach my athletes how to view the treadmill as a training tool so that when it is the best or only option there is an attitude of gratitude toward this beast of a machine. In fact, it is truly an excellent tool for measured intervals or incline work. The gym membership and my time spent running on the spot taught me a lot about gratitude.

I learned I could be grateful for circumstances that are not always ideal.

I still maintain an attitude of gratitude when needing to spend time on the treadmill or on an indoor bike. There is value in dialing in specific efforts on these controlled machines. And in the long, often slippery Wisconsin winters, I find value in being able to be safe and warm—and I get the opportunity to catch up on some shows on Netflix.

I didn't see how influential my time at the gym with Kylie was in finding my personal passion until much later in life. But after Ironman 2017 and then the Arizona 70.3 training cycle in 2018, I more than ever believe in the power of fully feeling able to honestly nurture passions while navigating the bigness of the rest of life simultaneously. I thrive on discovering my own passions, am drawn to watching them unfold in others, and feel compelled to help people find theirs when they are lost or undiscovered. At the same time, I have grown to stay content for longer with less searching and striving. In my younger years, I was impulsively led by reacting to emotions and passion. I grew up with a zeal for fun and was constantly seeking and repeating what felt good at that moment. Thankfully, as I have grown in wisdom and am surrounded by supportive people, I see the value in seeing the big picture as well as what is directly in front of me. I have found passion in the journey.

When I think of growing up with an excited spirit, I think of my youngest brother, Brendan. I am the oldest of four, with three younger brothers. My "baby" brother, Brendan, is seven years younger, but although he was truly a surprise to my parents, he has always been a huge gift to our family. Brendan exudes an energy for life. He is a present dad and husband, a loving son and brother, a smart and successful attorney, an avid sports fan, a great friend, and an influential member of his community. Brendan has always been and still is endearing and inspiring, and my relationship with him is invaluable to my life.

Brendan taught and still teaches me that you can live out your electrifying passion for all things.

We cannot ignore who we are, dumb it down, hide it to make others feel comfortable, and/or store it up and expect it to not burst out. We must not try to stay small or worry that we are "too much" for anyone. I fully believe that Brendan's ability to be unapologetically himself helped lead him to realizing what he wants in life, and he felt safe and secure enough to go for it without fear.

Now an adult, Brendan has built a life that he loves and allows him to live his passions every day. And his kids all have the same refreshing thrill for life, showing their excitement for the smallest joys, even though kids are constantly reminded of their need for the next bright and flashy thing by marketers. They have all turned into triathletes with my guidance and encouragement, and I hope they will find ways to live full human experiences, including fully living out their passions. I know Brendan and his wife, Sara, will model love and that their kids will have opportunities to live out their lives as whomever they need to be. And my hope is that they feel constantly electrified and inspire others to do the same.

HOW YOU CAN LEARN FROM ME

- Inspect your emotions with curiosity before reacting. Understand how reacting to excessive worry, guilt, resentment, and bitterness can remove you from the present moment and often zap passion.
- Focus on gratitude rather than longing for ideal circumstances. Seek out things, circumstances, and people to be grateful for, even among a desire for change.
- Find passion in the journey. You do not need to feel it positively pulsing through you in every moment for it to be real.
- Let your passion electrify you. When you have a zeal for life, don't be afraid to feel it and share it with others.

DO IT SCARED

At the end of the summer 2021, I signed up to race Ironman St. George on the day after my birthday in May 2022. I was riding pretty high on life at this time, taking on a "go for no" approach professionally, and it was serving me well. I was also excitedly preparing for a return to race the Ironman Arizona 70.3 in October, where I was aiming for a top-five finish and hoping to earn a qualifying slot to the 70.3 World Championship for 2022. I was seeking out hard things and thriving in the process. I recognized that I wanted a new, challenging athletic goal, and Saint George fit the bill on paper: full Ironman, unfamiliar course, cold water, hot air temp, and extremely hilly. And I would take on the winter, mostly indoor, training alone and then race without the comfort of my team. Hard, hard, and harder. And I was excited.

A couple of months later, Ironman announced this race would be one of two World Championship events held in 2022 to accommodate all the qualifiers who had been built up through the pandemic years. And while I didn't qualify, I was made aware that I was able to race alongside the best in the world since I had signed up before the decision was made. I could have opted out, but that didn't even seem like an option to me. Although I never tried to pretend that I qualified, I still knew I was worthy of showing up—I mean, we were there first, so technically the pros were borrowing our course.

As the race approached, I put the work in. I spent hours and hours on the indoor trainer, in the pool, and bundled up out on the road. I had the furthest reach on social media that I had ever had during an Ironman training cycle, and even though I was open and honest, people still assumed I had qualified. I knew this would be a hard Ironman for me to try to "race," and I started to feel very exposed. Even though I never doubted my ability to complete the race, which truly was my goal, I started to be consumed more by imposter feelings. Everyone thought I was going to "crush it," and rather than asking what that meant to them, I hid behind my fear. I fought my desire to compare myself to others and make myself a victim of well-intentioned friends and followers. When Jamie and I made the trip a few days before the race, I felt like I had overcome the battle. Rather than shy away from my nerves, I was going to just "do it scared."

I have not been to Kona, but the hype at Saint George didn't feel like what I imagined it to be on the Big Island. It was fun and manageable, thankfully adding value to my experience rather than reinforcing the feelings of being an imposter. I enjoyed most of the race lead-up, except the practice swim. I had been warned that the water was going to be cold, but fifty-seven degrees Fahrenheit felt like ice. We swam

750 meters, and I could feel myself getting colder the entire time and ended up shivering uncontrollably for a long time post swim, even in the eighty-five-degree air. I was not worried about the amount of climbing on the bike after driving the course beforehand. I believed I could manage the oppressive heat on the run. But I was damn scared of my ability to safely complete the swim two days later.

This fear mentally consumed me for almost forty-eight hours. I battled it mostly internally and shared some of it mildly on social media. I knew it wouldn't serve me to dwell on it, but it was still ever present. I quietly searched "signs of hypothermia" while Jamie wasn't around so I wouldn't appear to be overly worried. I even wondered if I should pull out of the race and enjoy watching the best in the world instead. And when I arrived at the race on Saturday, I watched the pros go off with a sense of fear and hope that I would exit the water safely. I was going to do it scared.

Long story short, my all-consuming fear did not do anything to serve me. As we approached the start line, Mike Reilly, the "Ironman voice," announced the water had warmed up to sixty-two degrees, and I was confident that although it would be chilly, it was doable. I had an expected swim and enjoyed every moment on the bike— well, maybe except the super windy and scary descent where people were getting blown off their bikes. I took in the beauty and remained grateful to be competing with the best in the most beautiful place. I learned much more during the run (more on that later), but I did finish the race with an exhausted smile.

The time spent succumbing to fear did not serve me, but it did not stop me. I decided I would do it scared.

I had fallen in love with the phrase "fear is a liar" in 2018 after realizing I had been following the loud voice of fear for way too long. Fear was driving my decisions and owning many of my relationships. It has often stopped me from hearing and trusting myself. It gives me anxiety, causes me to lash out, and frustrates me. While fear cannot be ignored, it can and should be challenged. Fear *lies* when it stops us from being real and authentic, and its loud voice speaks over the whispers of hidden or newly discovered goals and dreams. But I have learned that fears are often not what they appear to be on the outside.

Throughout my career, fear has crept up on me. As a coach, I started out fearful I would not be enough to take on my first Ironman athletes. I am forever grateful to Mac and Dave for giving me the opportunity to guide them on their Ironman journey, and for their grace and feedback. I learned much in the process, and I helped them get to the finish line. Nevertheless, when I make mistakes, I often allow fear to creep in and tell me I am not qualified enough to be a good coach. I know now that this is the fear of failure talking, telling me that I am an imposter. With more self-awareness and acceptance over the years, the voice of fear has become quieter and the voice of confidence louder. Although I commit to lifelong learning, I now identify as an expert coach specializing in mental training and life improvement through endurance sport. I am not afraid to make mistakes in order to move forward in my mission.

I am still afraid of many other things. My fear of snakes is almost always justified: snakes are creepy and slithery and unpredictable. The big ones can eat you whole, and some of the smallest can kill you with their venom. The truth is, I don't like snakes. But I am not afraid of all snakes killing me; I am afraid of the ones that could. Ultimately, it is a fear of the *unknown and not being in control of my surroundings*. I also have a fear of learning new technology, which is a pretty common one for many of us who are over thirty-five. In the winter of 2019, I had an incredible opportunity to coach our Zone racing team at an amazing cycling facility and was excited when I signed the contract and sold packages for our rides. I wholeheartedly believed it was a perfect fit for the team, but then I started to learn how much I had to learn about the high-tech facility and equipment. I realized I wasn't afraid of the new-to-me group smart-bike trainer setup or the technology that supported their use. I was afraid of *feeling exposed as foolish, being judged, disappointing people, and not being in control.* My third most potent fear applies to running an open 5K. I am not afraid of running in a crowd of racers, but I am afraid of running solo and not running fast enough to meet my expectations and those of others. I am afraid of the discomfort without an excuse. I am afraid of *failing and being judged.*

But I still do it scared. And I have learned that anticipatory fear is almost always worse than reality.

In the past, I have often defined certain people, circumstances, relationships, events, and goals as "frightening." I was afraid of being judged, misunderstood, unlikeable, irrelevant, unloved, and not belonging or living authentically. My fears subconsciously controlled me. They guided my thoughts, perceptions, and decisions. By resisting facing those fears head-on, I developed my biggest fear of all: that I wouldn't be able to give the world the real me, and therefore my family, friends, and humanity would not know how much I loved them.

I desired growth, so I sought to conquer some of these fears. I learned that things, people, or events are not overall categorized as scary. Our *perception* creates those ideas, and our resistance to challenging that perception keeps them there. I knew my biggest fears needed to be faced; I had to dig them out of the depths of myself. The thoughts that created the real fears were deeper than haunted houses, horror movies, or completing hard physical endeavors. Letting these deep-seated fears have any control in my life does not serve my purpose. So I asked for help with the things I feared. For example, each week at the cycling studio, I learned how to trouble-shoot the tech on my own; I have not and will not avoid certain areas because there might be snakes hiding in the grass; and I will run an open 5K when the opportunity arises.

Roughly ten years ago, I identified a real fear of dying without people knowing how much I loved those close to me, and all humanity. This was *scary*. I had to take a long and multifaceted look at this layered fear. After wrestling with it over several years, I understood that this fear was rooted in not fully giving my real self to the world. My energy for loving was being used on managing my persona. I still felt loads of love for people, but without loving myself, it was falling flat. I was letting my fears of not belonging, being rejected, and lacking control stop me from revealing my whole and real self.

I was causing my biggest fear to come true.

Through practice, I am able to see fear as the sneaky liar that it is. I have figured out how it likes to weave into my thoughts and get in the way of me being wholly alive. Now if I am afraid of doing something, I vow to try, at least once, to challenge my perception of its scari-ness. I won't allow fears of the unknown, a lack of control, failure, judgment, disappointing people, or looking foolish stop me from *knowing, believing in, or loving myself.* And I have also learned that when I live in the light of honesty, rather than in the darkness of fear, I am no longer afraid of loving. I believe I am *worthy* of being loved.

Recently, I decided to try a sport I had perceived many years ago as *uncomfortably scary*: mountain biking. My boys and husband love mountain biking. They value adventure and trying new things, and I admire this in them. I was interested in doing it but afraid the activ-ity wouldn't align with my natural abilities on a road bike and that I would be judged for my pace or nervousness. Finally, I took an oppor-tunity and tried it. I started slowly and carefully, and we didn't go far, but having survived it, I vowed to go again. I might not like it in the end, but first I had to face it head-on.

I will be honest about another ludicrous idea I had, one I really laugh about now. I fully blame the TLC show *A Wedding Story* for this, but I thought that once you met the "right" person you would have no more fears or insecurities. I met Jamie on October 13, 2001, and we were engaged in November the same year. In my opinion, and according to *A Wedding Story*, I was marrying the right person. Then, in March the following year, I found out I was pregnant with our first child, in May I graduated college, in June I began a new job, we got married in July, and in December our baby girl, Halle, was born. The following year I found out I was pregnant again in March, we bought a house and moved in July, in October I quit my job, and in November we had a baby boy. Jamie started a new job and worked literally one hundred hours a week opening a new restaurant only three days after I gave birth to Deaken. I got pregnant the next April and gave birth to Quinton the following February. I imagine this is hard for you all to keep up with—it is difficult for me to write it without getting tired. At twenty-four years old, I had three kids, plenty to learn, and no fear at all. I didn't think too much about loading up the double stroller, strapping on a baby carrier, and leashing up our two big dogs for a walk to the park. I moved forward the best I could, with youthful energy and confidence. This worked, until it didn't. Fears started to creep in: Was I a good enough wife and mother? Did our life resemble the idealistic *A Wedding Story*? Fear spoke the lies, and I started to believe and react to them. This led to a turbulent time in our marriage, one in which we grew through hardship. Worth mentioning, but not the topic of this book.

Fear can tell us many different kinds of lies that look and sound convincing. Fear can appear in our lives in the form of shame, the overwhelming desire to find comfort in perfectionism, busyness, martyrdom, and so on. Shame creeps in when we fail and tells us that we are not good enough anyway. Perfectionism forces us to strive for something we can never achieve. Busyness gives us a distraction and an inflated sense of importance, making us think we don't have time to consider our own needs, when it is really a cover story for fear.

Our brain craves stability, familiarity, and comfort. And our culture supports this. We are modeled on the idea that there is seemingly no fear in a comfortable life, so many people feel that reaching comfort is the pinnacle of living. Most of us value comfort on some level; we want to live in warm houses with enough food to fill our bellies while drinking safe water from our taps. But we also often end up making decisions that support short-term comfort rather than accepting temporary discomfort in order to follow through with our goals. We aim to stay in our comfort zone to stave off the fear of uncertainty in the unknown—discomfort, failure, missing out, being judged, and so on. The truth is, staying *within* the comfort zone requires a lot of work.

When safety is your driving force, you cannot always act on what you really want or who you truly are, because you need to act on what makes you feel the best in the moment.

I have been faced with my own desire for comfort many times, especially during races in my earlier career—the many I can recall when I "gave up" on myself and my goals. I realized I was not honoring my own values and instead making choices to safeguard my short-term comfort. So I wrote my values on a piece of paper and stuck it to my bathroom mirror, and now I intentionally make decisions from a place of love rather than fear. I am intent on applying this to my training as well. The other day while swimming hard, I put the thought *I don't value comfort* on repeat to keep pushing and challenging myself to be my best. I am glad that although it was a struggle, my fear, fueled by my desire for control, did not win over in the days leading up to the Ironman in Saint George. I am thankful I had experienced the power of doing things scared. This is a mantra I will continue using to help me reach my personal goals, help my athletes reach theirs, strengthen my relationships, and serve humanity in more impactful ways.

HOW YOU CAN LEARN FROM ME

- Face your fears intentionally. Do it scared if you need to.
- Set hard goals. It adds value to your life and builds character.
- Get uncomfortable. Don't settle within the comfort zone.

PART 2

GATHER TOOLS

Take a method and try it. If it fails, admit it frankly and try
another. But, by all means, try something.
FRANKLIN D. ROOSEVELT

CONNECT WITH YOUR MIND

IN 2019, AFTER MANY YEARS OF WRESTLING WITH PERSONAL, PRO-
FESSIONAL, AND ATHLETIC GROWTH, I was ready to take on a new and
very *real* stretch goal. I came to the realization that for many years of
racing I had been giving into the emotions around discomfort rather
than nurturing and listening to the voice that reminded me of my goal
and purpose. I had created the belief that, as a coach, I could not let my
athletes see me fail, and, in doing this, I was not authentically showing
up in my full experience; as such, I could not be an inspiration to my

athletes. After realizing this, I chose to train hard for the 2019 Ironman Wisconsin 70.3, with a goal of a top-five age-group finish.

I vulnerably voiced my goals to others, including on social media; I built up confidence through hard, lonely training sessions; I wrestled with the voice of my inner critic focusing on negative comparison, fear, and inadequacy; I visualized and practiced positive mantras; I trained my body; I aimed to train all parts of my mind—my strengths, my newly learned obstacles, my longtime default behavior patterns, and even my potential blind spots.

I was able to maintain focus in my head and a strong connection to the sensations in my body throughout the swim and bike portions, but I knew the run would present the biggest challenge: this was when the pressure of mental and physical exhaustion gave way to not only a weakened body but also a more vulnerable mind. I was able to run on trained autopilot for the first nine miles of the run, but then the anticipated thoughts started to creep in:

- *If you walk now, you might miss your overall goal, but it will still be a PR.*
- *You have tried so hard. No one will judge you.*
- *This hurts. So many others are walking. You can slow down. Or even walk a little.*
- *That's good enough.*

I had given in to my inner critic, letting these comfort-seeking thoughts dictate my effort many times before. I knew I had to maintain my mental focus to capture these thoughts, examine them, decide if they were true, and react. If not, I had to throw the thought away, like crumpling up a spoiled sheet of notebook paper. And then, on a new, clean sheet, I could rewrite the truth:

- *This is uncomfortable, and I am okay.*
- *I am inviting this discomfort. I expected it. It will not last forever.*
- *If I want to reach my goal, I will have to live with this discomfort until I reach the finish line.*

I had trained my mind and learned how my brain works and strives to help me feel more comfortable. I was able to keep wrestling with my strong desire to make it feel easier in the moment. I was *focused.* I couldn't even muster my standard smile when my close friends and family cheered me on. Instead, I was mentally and physically consumed by each painful step. I needed to use every ounce of energy to remind myself of the truth: *I want this. I can, and I will. I don't need comfort right now. I need to reach this goal.*

I crossed the finish line with a forty-minute personal record on the course and fourth in my age group. I rejoiced in my own mind and went on to enjoy the celebration with my family, friends, and teammates. My thoughts had controlled my actions, and by staying present, curious, and overall connected to these thoughts, I had pushed through perceived discomfort more than ever—and reached my goal.

The idea of connecting with my thoughts stemmed from a resource given to me by my most amazing mother-in-law. Candice has been a constant presence in my life since I married Jamie at the age of twenty-two. She has offered insight without judgment through the years, even when some of the most difficult things I have dealt with are conflicts within my marriage and her own son. In my more spiritually and emotionally immature days, I assumed that a part of her intention was to draw me away from my Christian faith and toward her own kind of spirituality. As I look back over these years, I now understand this is the opposite of true. She was growing in her own way, learning how to love others well, including her husband, who suffered relapse after relapse with his alcoholism. She eventually became a "spiritual director," a resource for believers of all faiths to understand, connect, and enrich their spiritual lives. My mother-in-law has taught me so many lessons through her quiet approach, one of them being the importance of "thought work" for daily peace in living in the present moment, no matter the circumstances.

I cannot recall when Candice gifted me the book *The Power of Now* by Eckhart Tolle. Neither can I recall what made me pick it up one day years ago and decide that I could get past some of the mystical spirituality and try some of the exercises for connecting with my thoughts, feelings, and actions. Despite my reservations, his practices were life-changing for me. I had prayed my entire life, focused on breathing, connected with my own voice and the feeling of a higher being, but I had never practiced thinking about my daily thoughts—of having a hyperawareness of why and how my brain was spinning. I decided to spend a lot of time "capturing my thoughts" and truly quieting my mind, sorting out the constant flow of thoughts that flooded it daily.

It was an exciting, horrifying, fun, and miserable process. I felt grateful that my thoughts were not scrolling on a ticker above my head for all to see, because as I practiced this, I began to understand how impactful they were in leading me to believe that I am an imposter in my own life. My own judgments of myself and others taught me a lot about why I struggled so much with fear and insecurity. The raw realness of how I thought showed me how much I was managing my persona rather than learning about myself. But through this practice, I was able to *connect with my own mind* and understand that believing in God didn't mean I was merely his puppet in the life that he gave me. My thoughts *mattered* to how I felt and lived.

So I continued to practice getting to know myself and what I really felt and believed rather than just having blind trust in doctrine. I thought *about my thoughts*, and when I spiraled into the desperate feeling of sadness, loneliness, or hopelessness, I could check in with more curiosity rather than continue to blindly validate all that I was thinking. I no longer feared my emotions, and now I am able to truly be in my own body. I am also better equipped to "capture" the lies and justifications of our culture, society, and even my own brain and privilege. Instead, I consider the thoughts through a lens of my values, morals, beliefs, and purpose. I can analyze them and choose how I want to change them or settle into discomfort when I cannot immediately change my circumstances.

This thought work helped me realize I had more impact on setting the tone for each day of my life, and I aimed to honor myself and my needs daily. I came to believe that it is harder to lie to myself when I journal my intentions each morning, and, when combined with reading Bible verses and praying, the practice has become my own kind of meditation that is vital to experiencing the realness of my days. This thought work and daily intentions guide the road map for my day-to-day interactions, as well as my training, racing, and coaching. I have learned through this practice how to stay true to what I really want and not let my busy mind give me excuses or outs, however justifiable they seem. Thought work helps me both nurture my soul and recognize when I am giving in to buffering or disconnection simply because it is hard. It helps me be more aware of potential areas where I still have so much to learn and practice. With this practice, I can return to the morning's truth and stay present in a difficult conversation with an athlete, go one more lap in the pool, or stay on the road longer. I can also open my eyes to the ugliest parts of the world with more compassion while simultaneously working for change.

One foundational practice I often include when setting intentions for my day is expressing gratitude. This is very different from focusing on gaining perspective—that is, reminding myself that "things could always be worse." Focusing on what I am grateful for softens my heart toward myself and others and enables me to see the world through a hopeful lens. There have been so many mentors in my life that have encouraged me to practice daily gratitude, including Candice, my friends Bella and Molly (more about them later), and many of the mentors I have had through the years. Focusing on gratitude for the day combined with being grateful for the ability to put my body to a major test has encouraged me through each of my Ironman competitions. I even made a chart detailing my nutrition and hydration strategies, and a list of roughly sixty people to give thanks for over the 112 miles. Logistical benefits aside, this list of people was more than just a distraction; it was a reminder of how grateful thoughts can serve me, even during (invited) moments of physical discomfort. That gratitude turned the experience into a communal one during those lonely times on the bike. I believe having a realistic and grounded "attitude of gratitude" can add value to your daily life, even when you're experiencing the darkest times. And this starts with understanding your thoughts.

HOW YOU CAN LEARN FROM ME

- Focus on your thoughts to start connecting with yourself on a deeper level.
- Stop believing all thoughts are automatically true. Question your thoughts. Explore what makes you think them and why you believe they are true. Create results rather than reactions.
- Keep a daily intention journal. Understand that your thoughts

control your feelings, and your feelings dictate your actions. When you can honestly set intentions in your life, you will have the ability to feel the full enjoyment of completing your objectives.

- Create grateful thoughts. Find things to be grateful for, even in times of struggle. You can be suffering and grateful at the same time.

STAY VULNERABLE

I was fortunate to have a fabulous running partner for a few years. Paula and I covered many miles together every Saturday morning, through sun, rain, cold, and snow. In October 2016, we both trained for and ran the Lakefront Marathon in Milwaukee. I had a great day with a significant marathon personal record. Paula had a rough day, but she still finished. I encouraged her to join me in signing up for our first ultramarathon: the MadCity 50K in April 2018.

Our long runs together and our "therapy chitchat" deepened our special friendship bond. The pace was slightly easier for me, and when Paula would start to tire, questioning her ability, I would easily fall into the role of encourager. And then Paula's normal running fatigue started to turn into actual pain in her hip. As a coach, I strongly encouraged her to stop running if she was unable to walk afterward. In hindsight, we both recognized she should have stopped running long before she did in order to take care of her body, but I also know how hard this is to do when you love to run—and if you are reading this book, you likely understand that as well. Sadly, the pain eventually became too hard to handle, even for a very strong woman like Paula, and her body gave in to the injury. She pulled out of the training and knew she wouldn't race. I absolutely agreed with the decision and was happy she was going to focus on her (long) process of healing. I would miss our long training runs and the connection of sharing the experience, but I was not aware of how much my encouraging Paula was only serving me, not her. Paula's training had become a buffer to my own vulnerability. I distinctly remember making my coffee in my Girl Strong coffee mug the morning before my first long run alone for the 50K training cycle. Feelings of despair, worry, and nervousness overtook my typical excitement. I became acutely aware of the task at hand, and even though I had run several marathons and completed Ironman races, I was suddenly not only afraid of covering the distance alone but also of doing it at all. But I laced up my shoes and headed out anyway, carrying my fear and worry along with me. I spent many hours training alone over several weeks and was fortunate to have other friends join in for some segments of my longest runs. Paula became my biggest encourager. I arrived at that start line stronger not only in body but also in mind. I ended up running a successful race on an unseasonably cold day the following April, cheered on by my family, Paula, and many team members.

Recognizing the need for more personal vulnerability was very timely coming off the Ironman experience of 2017. It solidified a message I had been receiving through many avenues for a few years: if I want to be wholly present in my life, I had to first know myself better and then be more vulnerable and open to failure. I had taken the natural role of encourager to another level, letting it become a cocoon of protection around me that stopped me from figuring out my own hard lessons. I had identified what I was doing, and the 50K experience helped me see the why. I desired to focus on being more vulnerable in all of life, especially in relationships—starting with myself.

I am very fortunate to have been mentored by many fabulous

women. This was not always the case, and I had to learn about myself and relationships through a lot of painful trial and error. I did not fully trust women, a distrust possibly rooted in an incident way back in middle school. In 2018 I would have never considered that a "mean girl" incident at the end of fourth grade could have a significant impact on my life, but years later I was able to acknowledge how much it likely did.

In 1989 I won "Artist of the Year," and during post–award ceremony recess, my group of girlfriends sent a representative to tell me that they didn't want to be friends with me anymore. Since it was the last day of school, we were released early, and I was able to run home to cry in my mom's arms. I was confused and devastated. When my mom took my brothers and I to the local Hardee's for an end-of-year ice cream cone, we saw the group of friends who had just dumped me. I still remember my mom looking them all in the eyes and telling them how mean it was for them to do something like that to a friend. This "mother bear" moment resonated with me as an example of strength—she did not attack them or their character but kept it about the incident and assessed it honestly. My mom modeled confidence in her words and actions, being a loving and safe protector. Although she chose to focus on the all-consuming task of raising four kids instead of putting the time needed to grow deep female friendships, I am forever thankful for the things she did to model and teach me.

Ultimately, I had a fun-filled summer making new neighborhood friends and enjoying the freedom from trying to impress or fit in with a group that was a dictatorship based on the insecurities of the leader. It taught me how to adapt and move on in courage and security. The time spent with this hodgepodge group of different ages and sexes also taught me to learn to love people for who they are in that exact moment. But those moments still leave an impression on a young girl, so when I started looking at my relationships later in life, I realized I never really processed those feelings that accompanied the rejection I experienced in fourth grade.

After the rejection, and having grown up with three younger brothers, I found it easier to forge male friendships. I love honesty, directness, sports, and immature humor, which I associated with male relationships. I hate gossip, backstabbing, and drama, and, in my mind, these things defined female relationships. I am very thankful for the lessons my three brothers and multitude of male friends taught me and for making it easy for me to connect with men in relationships today. The confidence I have in this arena gives me the ability to lead a team and coach many talented, influential, respected male athletes. I am able to see men for who they are and gain their trust, which enables me to help them be the best athletes they can be. Although this is true, I also realized I was also taking the path of least resistance in friendship. I was able to connect with male friendships on more of a surface level, and that felt less scary than putting my heart into more "dangerous" friendships with women. But then I desired to grow close with a couple of amazing women, and when conflict or discomfort arose, I was ill equipped to be vulnerable and honest as the relationships changed and evolved.

I learned many of my relationship lessons through my friendship with Ella, a fellow runner and triathlete. Like Kylie, I also met Ella through taking our young kids to the gym's Kids' Club day care early in the morning. Ella seemed to be perky in all aspects of life. In all honesty, I was at a low when I met Ella and living in such a state of insecurity and unidentified loneliness that I had probably been too intimidated to spark up a conversation. Ella and her husband, Jay, accepted and befriended me, basically adopting the kids and me while

Jamie worked long hours each night. We shared dreams and experiences, including going to events, outings, and competing in many races. Ella showed up and ran-walked as I vomited my way through the last 10K of my first marathon, while Jamie ran the rest with Jay. Ella had boundless energy, and we had many adventures with and without the kids. Ella opened up to me, and I can remember honest conversations that were shocking to me at the time, but now I see the *real vulnerability* in her openness.

Ella and Jay ended up moving to another city in Wisconsin when we moved to Oregon, Wisconsin. She struggled to fit in and find friends, and I felt alive and excited to be in what I considered the place where we would raise our kids and watch them grow and thrive. As she experienced her own evolution, she identified new values. It became clear that, as her values shifted and she sought out her new passions, we didn't connect as we had in the past. Whenever she reached out and opened up, I felt the relationship to be draining and more like a chore. Instead of being honest and vulnerable in a way that could've honored truth and love, I pulled away and treated her in a way that I would never want to be treated—with indifference. I told myself and others that her lack of love for her husband and desire to be a full-time mom meant we were growing apart, which in some ways we were, but the long-term investment in the friendship was worth my vulnerability.

At this time of my life, this confession about Ella is a very hard thing for me to write. Looking at events through a different lens, I now see that when I pulled away from her it was because of her raw vulnerability during her time of growth, my resistance to it, and my own inability to be vulnerable. Unfortunately, her exploration of a new set of values, combined with my fears, did not yield a continued friendship. But Ella taught me about the importance of vulnerability for connection and for respect of others in relationships. I am not proud of the way I handled it, especially at the end, but I am grateful for her friendship, the connection we shared in our physical goals, the fun memories, and the lessons I had to learn.

In hindsight, my relationship with Ella taught me many things about myself. When I met Katie at the tail end of my friendship with Ella, I was still learning how to have better female friendships. As it often happens when learning big lessons in life, my pendulum had swung all the way to almost brutal honesty. I was drawn to Katie for many of the same reasons I was drawn to a friendship with Ella. We have kids close in age, and we enjoy athletic endeavors, including racing. But Katie was all the way on the other end of the spectrum when it came to the ability to be open and vulnerable. I seemed to think it would be easier for me to help fix her rather than walk away with another failed friendship on my record. Guess what? This didn't work, and I spent almost a full year managing my friendship with Katie. I was honest and made my best attempt at being vulnerable. We were backyard neighbors and training partners, and we shared many fun experiences, but she couldn't reciprocate the vulnerability. She would lie to me openly, attempt to manipulate situations and other mutual relationships, and would speak negatively about me to others often. And then Katie would choose to play the victim, even when I would directly tell her what I needed and why I was pulling away. This relationship could not be sustained, but it did have a big impact on me and taught me more about my own vulnerability.

After grieving the loss of another friend, whom I had hoped could align with my core values, I saw more clearly what these values are and set boundaries to adhere to them. I solidified my "deal break-ers"—honesty, kindness, trustworthiness—and became willing to walk away from the other person when needed. I have also learned the importance of communicating with truth *and love* in order to better serve others while expressing my own needs. And best of all, these lessons have enabled me to connect deeply with some women on a foundation of honesty and vulnerability and see when our values misalign so that our relationship can shift or end with honesty and grace.

When I raced Ironman Wisconsin 70.3 in 2019 for the top-five age-group finish, I was able to test how much I could allow myself to vulnerably feel. Although I had competed well in fifteen 70.3 races, three full Ironmans, and hundreds of smaller races, this was a stretch goal for me and required a huge personal record on the course. I trained hard and continued to capture my thoughts. My mantra became, "Is this really hard enough? Do you have more to give?" I trained mostly alone, not entering the comforting place of putting the well-being of others ahead of my own goals. It was hard, and sometimes sad and lonely. When it came to the race, I was ready for whatever the day had to offer. I had always given up in my mind during the run, allowing my talent on the bike to shine and then come up with various excuses as to why my run was or was not the best that day. This time was different. I ran hard and felt the familiar pain creep in and then overtake my legs at about mile ten. I was vulnerable and exposed. I had to face the pain and run with it and settle with whatever place I landed in after most likely watching the other women pass me. I wrestled with the decision for a few minutes and then chose to be okay with it. For the final three miles of the run, I chanted, "This is pain, and pain is okay. This is what I expected to feel, and I will be okay." This pain was evident in my facial expressions to my friends who rode alongside to cheer me on, including my fiercely loyal friend Kelli. I got to lean on her, and she didn't distract me but loved me with empathic encouragement. And I felt it.

Now I know that vulnerability is the key to true connection in life—to oneself and to others. It can be scary, and it is always imperfect, but I know it has helped me be a better wife, mom, friend, coach, and athlete.

HOW YOU CAN LEARN FROM ME

- Don't hide behind others in order to protect your vulnerability.
- Communicate with loved ones from a place of vulnerability, truth, and love. For yourself and for them. Vulnerability is the key to belonging within yourself and with others.
- Own your mistakes in life. Being vulnerable includes a willingness to see your own flaws and negative contributions to relationships.

LIVE IN BOTH/AND

As I have already mentioned, I ran my first open marathon in Milwaukee, Wisconsin, in October 2007. If you have been in the US racing world that long, you'll most likely remember this as the day record-breaking heat caused the death of one runner and the cancellation of the Chicago Marathon. I started my race at 7:00 a.m. in seventy-five degrees Fahrenheit and sweltering humidity. Ella's husband, Jay, and I planned to navigate the course together, both feeling well trained and aiming to run the race in under four hours.

At the halfway point, I wasn't feeling as well as I had on most training runs. I was suffering from side aches, which wasn't a typical ailment. I was focusing on hydration, taking on more fluids than I have ever trained with and using gels for nutrition. At mile fifteen, I started to feel queasy and vomited on a lawn somewhere around Grafton and again by the lake at mile seventeen. Jamie and Ella were traveling the course alongside us in a car. After the second vomiting incident, they pulled ahead and parked, preparing to run the final eight-plus miles with us—Jamie with Jay and Ella with me. I wished Jay good luck, sending him off with Jamie, who ran alongside Jay in his sandals and cargo shorts.

I ended up having quite a journey. Ella and I part walked, part jogged more than eight miles, with stops for intense vomiting alternating with attempts to get some fluid back inside my failing body. It was miserable and, in hindsight, very dangerous. Ella was an amazing friend, doing all she could to encourage me to keep moving forward. I appreciated her very much, and I ended up crossing the finish line in a little more than five hours. I was seriously dehydrated and didn't go to the bathroom for nearly eighteen hours after the race. It was not smart or something I would ever encourage anyone to do. But I did finish.

I know now I should have found medical attention on the course or visited the medical tent postrace. I was severely hyponatremic— needing sodium and electrolytes, which cannot be found in the plain water I was guzzling out on the course. I was ignorant, but I was young, so I have not suffered any long-term effects of these decisions. I was thankful for Ella taking pictures and chitchatting when I could pull it together enough to engage, but now I understand how disconnected and distracted I was to what my body was telling me. This all taught me that distractions are not innately bad, but it is very important to be aware of how you use them in your life. At times allowing an intentional and short reprieve from the heaviness of life is helpful to reset. But it is helpful to think of this as more of a both/and approach rather than the either/or. I could have benefitted from looking outward for some laughs and distraction while also looking inward often to ensure my personal safety. This strategy can be applied in racing and in all of life to make sure you don't continue to avoid the root causes of problems and spiral out of control, not fully living with awareness—and potentially ending up with kidney failure!

One of my most acute moments of witnessing the need to live in the both/and was through the life and death of my friend Margie. I met Margie through my friend Kelli in 2014. They had been long-time friends, and Margie, her husband, Blake, and their two little girls were moving back to Wisconsin after a stint working for Nike in Portland, Oregon. Blake's brother, Mark, was also Kelli's brother-in-law—married to her beautiful sister, Reese. Margie was diagnosed with breast cancer almost immediately after moving to Wisconsin—into a small apartment while waiting for their new home to be built just up the street from us in Oregon, Wisconsin. After the devastating diagnosis, Kelli called me in to help with some nutritional advice, and I was able to help Margie figure out an eating plan as she went through her first round of treatment. She was sick and bald but still the same charismatic woman with one of the most infectious personalities you could ever encounter. She got the all-clear thumbs-up after chemo. But sadly, within a very short time, the cancer came back in her liver. A stage four terminal cancer diagnosis at thirty-nine years old. The shock waves of this news rocked her close family and friends and made its way to acquaintances. Everyone knew her as a fighter.

She tried treatments and drug trials, but as fucking cancer does, it beat her down and made her sicker and sicker. Kelli was a devoted friend to Margie always, but her loyalty really shone during this time. She would lie there for hours with her, watching episodes of *Pit Bulls & Parolees*. She delivered sub sandwiches. She was strong for Margie and Blake and the girls. She was strong for her sister (and Margie's sister-in-law), Reese. She was strong for her own girls when they were scared.

I watched all of this unfold while offering all I could from a place of not having known Margie for long but wanting to know her better and to help. I delivered smoothies and took every opportunity that was offered to visit or tag along on the rare occasion she felt up to going out. I sent my love and support to Blake. I felt mostly helpless, until slowly I found a way. I made it my mission to support my strong friend Kelli. I knew she had to be struggling with the weight of all she was carrying, and so I offered to listen and in doing so take some of the burden from her. No doubt she loved Margie, and she stayed strong to show her love to everyone despite being so scared inside. Like everyone else involved, she didn't want to lose her friend. I listened to Kelli when she couldn't be vulnerable in front of others. I provided distractions to her fear and sadness when she needed moments to let go. I let her vent and cry and laugh whenever she needed to. I encouraged her to live in the both/and as a loving, positive friend and also as a hopeless and terrified woman. I hope I was a good friend to her during this time, and I believe Margie's loved ones benefitted from me loving Kelli so that she could keep soldiering on. Sadly, Margie died on Kelli's fortieth birthday, three months after her own.

From her rigor for life to the lesson that you never know when your time on this earth will be up, Margie taught me that every day matters.

Living in the idea of both/and was as important at this time in Kelli's life, as it was for me to cross the finish line in 2007. She needed light times to offset the heaviness of the darker ones. She needed to think about herself while looking out to care for so many.

Margie's husband, Blake, taught me so much about living in both/and through our life-changing conversations following Margie's death.

Blake taught me that gratitude and grief can exist simultaneously in your body, heart, and mind.

He vulnerably shared his raw pain of grief while also feeling overwhelmed with joy, love, and gratitude whenever he felt the tenderness of a friend reaching out or his young girls enjoying their passions. His words, and the realness of his experience, reached me in a way that changed not only how I looked at grief but also how I looked at all things in life.

Years later, when experiencing the sometimes-daily losses and burdens associated with the COVID-19 global pandemic, I was able to remember this message. I was at peace with my heart in two pieces, one side mourning and acknowledging the financial, physical, emotional, and mental struggles of humanity, and the other bursting with gratitude for my health, my home, extra time with my husband and teenagers, and a slower pace to think and breathe. I stopped focusing on the fear in the media and started looking within, realizing that life is not this *or* that. Life is this *and* that.

HOW YOU CAN LEARN FROM ME

- Be aware of distractions or "buffers." Give yourself some occasional breaks, but don't be afraid to feel, even the negative emotions.
- Be there for friends during hard times. Support and encourage their own healing, and encourage them to live in the both/and.
- Embrace the process. Endurance racing allows for heightened body awareness. Focus on how you are acclimating to the rigors of prolonged and/or intense exercise. While

headphones, friends, or pretty scenery can help you get through miles and miles of training, they can be distractions on race day. Learn to alternate looking out and looking within.

- Be present. Don't be afraid of any feelings. You are capable of letting them flow through you.

FEEL IT ALL

I am a "lifestyle" racer, but currently not a lifestyle full-Ironman distance athlete. Training and competing in triathlons or running races has been part of my daily life since my first race in 2007. But I have always benefited from an extra nudge in my soul to take on the nine months or more of training for the full-distance race. In the fall of 2012, after two years owning the Zone Fitness and Training gym, I decided it was time to give my faithful members a glimpse into the training and racing process of an Ironman triathlete. The (mostly) women members inspired me every day with their commitment and hard work to their fitness regimen. Most of them were not yet triathletes, but ass-kickers in personal training sessions and in all group fitness classes, including group cycling, boot camps, strength training, or whatever else I created for them to try. I had great appreciation for them and wanted to inspire them to keep dreaming. So, in September 2012, I got in line, paid my fee, and excitedly set forth on another long training journey.

I didn't know this road would be much bumpier than in 2009, the last time I conquered this goal. At the time, I felt that my why was concrete ("inspiration," as I called it then). I wanted to *inspire the members of the Zone to believe that anything is possible*. But my training was unfocused and lonely. Soon after signing up for the race, I gave in to financial turmoil and personal exhaustion and sold the Zone to my good friend Kelli. Although I felt fortunate to be working there, and with a huge added benefit of earning a paycheck for the first time in a couple of years, I realize now that I had not grieved the loss of my business. As I have mentioned, I had learned to be resourceful with my feelings, only spending a short time allowing vulnerability before moving on with feigned strength. This way of navigating hard times had been modeled by my parents, and I relied on it throughout my young adult life by taking care of three kids whose ages spanned a mere two and a half years. By 2013, I had also learned how to manage my outward persona, bury or distract myself from negative emotions, and generally keep up the appearance that I had it together while working doubly hard to do what needed to be done. I was exhausted and emotionally fragile, trying to avoid grieving a loss and manage both a new job and rigorous training schedule, all while being a present parent and a loving, supportive wife.

In the spring of 2013, Jamie decided it was time to fulfill his goal of building and opening a new restaurant in our community of Oregon, Wisconsin. He had been in the hospitality industry since I met him, and we were already the owners of a successful bar and grill in a neighboring city. I believed in him and supported his decision. But having been down this road before, I had the festering reminder that the physical and emotional commitment to his work would likely tear him away from the family for a period of time. I struggled to communicate my fears to him clearly. He secured investors and started the project. And then hurdles and roadblocks beyond imagination began to surface. Circumstances beyond our control caused the building process to come to a halt. We weren't sure the restaurant could be completed, even with tens of thousands of dollars already invested.

The risk was suddenly very apparent, and our financial future felt uncertain. The stress caused Jamie to retreat and become emotionally, mentally, and physically unavailable. He had an uncharacteristic panic attack and then came down with shingles. I wanted to be loving and compassionate, but I was too busy distracting myself from the grief of my own business loss. I turned inward and became bitter and selfishly driven. I was frustrated, lonely, and intent on sharing all the ways I was a victim in the situation. I acted out of guilt and resentment rather than love and support. We were in a cycle in which we turned on each other rather than loving each other. Our marriage suffered, and I was faced with a choice to stay or go.

My training was my one outlet, but as you can likely guess, it was still lackluster. I put all my energy into appearing to be a peppy coach and trainer, a present mom, and a soon-to-be two-time Ironman finisher. But in reality, I was suffering. It was getting harder and harder to *manage* my circumstances rather than fully *feel* all the emotions that were demanding more and more attention. My passion fizzled as my energy was funneled into blaming my husband for the stress and fear of financial uncertainty, and even more importantly, my marriage ending. When my passion dissipated, my perception of the goal dissolved as well.

The why remained the same, but inspiring others felt unattainable when I was managing the perception of my life rather than being honest with myself and others.

The short-story ending to this story is that through marriage therapy and my own self-care work, Jamie and I were able to reconnect and eventually became stronger than ever. He persevered, and we opened Headquarters Bar and Grill in February 2014 and still serve the Oregon community today. And I crossed the Ironman finish line in 2013 after a rough bout of dehydration, fueled by the amazing support of so many friends, family members, athletes, and Zone members. I was excited to have another finisher medal, and I believe I inspired many. During the training process and beyond, I learned how important it is to let yourself fully and openly grieve and feel. As women, our culture often encourages us to be gracious supporters, but we must be aware of crossing the line into ignoring our own needs. And then, to fully feel the celebration of realizing our goal, we need to not only give our physical time but also be willing to give mental and emotional energy to grieve in order to feel the full joys of success.

When you spend a lot of time focusing on the idea that your thoughts control your feelings, and your feelings control your actions, you can start to believe that the main goal is to cultivate a consistently positive mindset. That is most definitely not the secret to a full and content life. If you exist only in your own head and focus only on positivity, you run the risk of missing most of your life, including the good parts. You become self-absorbed and unavailable to others because your energy gets diverted into *managing yourself* rather than accepting what you are feeling and acting from that reality. Resisting negative feelings leads to more pain and often suffering.

Life is not all good or all bad. It's fifty-fifty.

In 2015 Jamie and I shared a race experience that spanned the gamut of feeling. We decided to bond over training and racing a marathon together and chose Rails to Trails, a race that follows a flat railroad path through a beautiful location in central Wisconsin. We ran every long run together, shuffling along on different paths, enjoying conversation and sharing pain. It was a fun process, and I look back on the training fondly, even the emergency bathroom stops, sometimes in the woods—thankfully, we could and always can laugh it off later.

When the race approached, he and I agreed to run together until one of us began to lag behind, and then we would leave each other to encourage the other to go on to their best race possible. At this time I had been visiting a holistic doctor to help treat some of my recurring stomach issues (see earlier comment about bathroom stops!) and was on a pretty strict elimination diet. In hindsight, this probably wasn't the smartest thing to do right before a big endurance event, but you know what they say about hindsight.

We drove to my parents' cabin, prepped our dinner, and woke up early to take on the short drive to the race site. We stayed together for the first five or six miles, and then I started to feel a bit off. My body felt sore, tight, and almost robotic. In hindsight, looking through my coaching lens, I can see I had not been eating enough carbohydrates in training and definitely not in the days leading up to the race. Jamie went ahead of me, and I kept trudging along, feeling the tightness in my hips increasing. He had his own issues, needing a bathroom break, so I passed him. He came upon me at mile eighteen, and I was in some serious pain and discomfort. I felt as if I couldn't get any range of motion out of my hips and was near tears, thinking that for the first time ever I was going to have to quit a race. He tried to encourage me. I resisted the encouragement and started to get angry. We started having a more heated conversation while both shuffling along. At one point I needed to get away from his cheerfulness and started to shuffle faster. And then I did all I could to stay in front of him, motivated by my own unnecessary anger with him, which was nothing more than frustration with my situation. I finished the race, and so did he, after me. This race was filled with negative emotion that I was forced to physically feel in the moment. It was mentally defeating when I couldn't run the race I wanted and then emotionally defeating when I lashed out at him. In the end, it was also rewarding to get through such acute feelings while trying to cover 26.2 miles. Luckily, I apologized, and we were able to hug, laugh, and head home to celebrate, after only mildly arguing more about who would drive back to the cabin with dead legs. We eventually made it home safely, napped, and had some burgers and beers (who can do an elimination diet post-marathon?). We still laugh about that mess of a race and see it as a time when feeling it all wasn't easy but yielded a full experience.

HOW YOU CAN LEARN FROM ME

- Live authentically by honoring your feelings, not managing your persona.
- Communicate how you feel with your loved ones. Tell them how you feel in real time rather than letting them sort out your reactions.
- Accept that life is fifty-fifty. Life is a big picture, full of many different emotions, arguably 50 percent of what we consider "positive" emotions and 50 percent "negative." No one can and will feel happy all the time, but you can feel more content by embracing how you truly feel.
- Don't hold on to feelings when they pass. Holding grudges doesn't harm the other person or the circumstances. It hurts you most.

KNOW WHY

As I mentioned previously, Ironman 2017 set off not only a light bulb but also a series of flashy fireworks I could not ignore. I believe the timing meant I could be less a victim of circumstances. The overall positivity of the experience helped me to see it as an opportunity for growth rather than being upset about the outcome personally. The problem wasn't that I had set the "wrong goal" or had a "bad why." The reason I felt disconnected and flat after the race was that I hadn't fully given myself to my purpose. Although I was experiencing success in leading others to their goals, I was still wrestling with people-pleasing, comparison, dishonesty with myself, and lack of self-worth. So I made choices that honored other *whys* along the way. I was divided, training to prove I could be successful, a.k.a. fast, rather than joining my friends and athletes for the immersive experience of it with them. Therefore, I missed out on the *full* experience of success and bonding that was available to me. The tiny thing that was missing reflected a bigger obstacle in my life, one that I was ready to tackle with full force.

This idea of having a why, a purpose, a passion, a curiosity—or whatever you would like to call it—is not a new concept. But it has made its way into mainstream thinking through the prevalence of podcasts and social media. It is easy to pick up the message that "your life is emptier than it needs to be without a driving passion." While I do agree that each goal is better actualized with the awareness of the purpose, I think staying curious is better than defeat for figuring out your why. So, if you don't know your purpose, learn more and hope that through trial and error you will find one. And then be aware and open to the idea of it continually changing. The point is to try and learn from successes *and* failures, not be driven by the urgent need to arrive at a brilliant purpose. But nor should you blindly go through life without a road map at all.

The documentary *Free Solo* is an intimate portrait of rock climber Alex Honnold as he prepares to achieve his lifelong dream of free solo climbing, without a rope, one of the world's most famous rocks: El Capitan in Yosemite National Park, California. Unbelievably, he climbs the mostly sheer face of a giant rock alone, without any safety gear. Honnold's unique brain chemistry aids him in making decisions that could very easily cost him his life. I found the science complex yet fascinating, but what drew me in the most was the borderline-arrogant way he told the audience that he had to do it to feel *alive*. He knows himself and why he needed to climb that rock; it was the only thing he could do *to feel whole and complete*. His passion spoke so loudly that it would drown out everything else for the rest of his life if he didn't fulfill it. He knows his why.

Like Alex, I had to believe in my inherent worthiness in order to be inspired to find my purpose again. Sometimes your passion shows up and the why becomes clear when faced with death and deciding to fight. I met Sara in 2010, when I was getting ready to purchase the local gym. She and her husband, Rand, were prominent members of the community and vocal in giving me advice for success. They seemed skeptical of my abilities as a business owner, but they agreed to stay on as members and came to many of my classes weekly. I formed a wonderful friendship with them, and I respect them greatly. Even though they were a couple of the oldest participants in my cardio-intense strength, cycling, and boot camp classes, they showed up and gave it their all, which inspired everyone in the group. Sara and Rand, along with another amazing gym member, Janie, taught me that age is not an excuse to set easy goals. If you have arrived in your comfort zone, you have stopped truly living.

When Sara was diagnosed with breast cancer in 2013, we were all shocked. She did not fit the description of someone who would get cancer. She was energetic, youthful, healthy, strong, and basically badass. This was my first introduction to the truism that "anyone can get cancer." I am not the naivest person to walk this earth, nor do I live in a cave, but I had never been faced with such a healthy person getting such a life-rocking diagnosis. We rallied behind Sara.

She had a brief stint of believing she was cancer-free, and then it came back as metastatic cancer, commonly known as stage four. Sara had to decide how she would navigate her battle with cancer and chose to keep making big goals—even though no one would fault her for giving in to a woeful, more self-driven existence. Rather, she became an advocate, and she has raised hundreds of thousands of dollars for a local cancer research center. She wrote an inspiring blog that detailed her journey, a blog that was real and honest, filled with humor. She not only found the strength within herself to fight but also to set goals while doing so. She still fights today. Sara abandoned some of her short- and long-term goals to make new goals: not only to fight to live but to fight to bring awareness and ultimately more funding to the very underrepresented cause of metastatic breast cancer. One of her campaigns that reflects her goal-crushing ability is to swim across lakes. I had the honor of joining her in the summer of 2015 in swimming across six local lakes with her amazing support system of friends and fellow Oregonians and gym members. It was a blessing to just swim alongside her, but the true inspiration was in her raw and honest speech that she gave before each swim. Her why was clear, and her purpose unwavering. She fought for herself while fighting harder for future generations of women and men who would be affected by metastatic breast cancer. Sara always had a passion for justice, and it is very inspiring to watch her funnel this passion into saving the lives of future girls, boys, women, and men. Sara and my friend Margie taught me that no matter the circumstances, goals are worth setting, and when you have a clear purpose, *every day matters*. This inspiration has taken on new shapes as I have grown and evolved as a female athlete and coach.

As you know, fitness and endurance racing became my experiment for finding my life purpose—my why. I had to train and race for years while making many mistakes in all aspects of my life. My journey to a personal hobby and career in the industry started in 2007, but my 2017 Ironman hindsight opened my eyes more fully to all the lessons I had learned and applied through this self-growth vehicle. *Ten years* of participating, learning, succeeding, failing, mentoring, growing, falling, and being shunned, ignored, celebrated. I am not sure if I am a slow learner, but I am thankful for the grace to learn many lessons along the way.

One of my biggest realizations, regarding how hard it is to succeed without a strong why, came after the Door County Half Ironman in 2011. No matter how hard I think back on this race, I cannot think of any defined purpose for taking it on. I believe my motivation was a blurry combination of having done it before, the fact that others were doing it, Door County being a fun place to visit, and it giving me something to do. A fine set of *reasons*, but not a purpose that drove my interest in training hard leading up to the race. So I barely trained. I didn't seek out ways to manage the heat better. I hadn't officially trained as a coach yet and went into the experience as a somewhat arrogant athlete. But I was hit with a huge dose of reality. At a heat index over one hundred degrees, that day literally was *steaming*. My race was a mess from the beginning. The swim was in choppy water, as is often the case in Lake Michigan, and I had plenty of time to consider my lack of preparation and even thought about pulling out of the race entirely. In an effort of fake toughness, I kept going. I banked my first excuse in my mind: "The water was so tumultuous this year!"

My bike time was slower than usual for me, and I started to rehearse my second excuse for the day—the weather: "This is unreasonable. It is too hot. They are telling people to stay indoors. We are stupid and stubborn. We are harming ourselves. We could literally *die*." And this was my mantra for the *entire* run. A little over thirteen miles of crabby, angry, excuse-making vitriol that caused me to lash out at anyone who cheered, smiled, or told me I was "looking good." Did they not understand how stupid it was to compete today?

I finished, and I was happy. Happy to be *done*. After some reflection, however, I realized I was miserably stuck in a rut of thinking I was a naturally good triathlete, who didn't need to train and deserved perfect racing conditions. And I truly *was* a good athlete, but I lacked some of the attributes needed to *stay* a good athlete. I made the excuses through the stories I heard and told myself, although the truth was I had no why. I vividly remember telling myself I was either going to "do this right" the next time, or I was done. It ended up being a pivotal moment in my career and life. I decided that although I didn't have all the answers, I would at least have one reason for racing. It is clear to me now that this is when I decided each race would have an *inspiration*.

From that race forward, I only signed up for races with some kind of purpose in mind. I still faltered with 100 percent follow-through, and often the reason was that I wasn't fully honest with myself. But it was a solid start, and one I needed before becoming a coach myself. I could share a story from every race after that moment, detailing the successes and failures of my training and racing in relation to the validity of the purpose I had defined for that goal.

I hope it has been clear that the important thing is to know, understand, trust, and be honest with yourself when establishing your goals and whys for each goal. It does not always have to be tackled with great ferocity or a narrow, individual focus, but it has to be clear.

In 2016 I decided I wanted to give back to the sport of running in a more obvious way. I recruited a couple of runner friends, and we signed up to participate in the Madison half-marathon with myTEAM TRIUMPH, a company that gives physically or mentally disabled individuals a race experience. I took my youngest son, Quinton, with me to the practice runs, where we had to learn how to navigate and (most importantly) stop the large cart that our new "captain" Jake would ride in for the duration of the race. Quinton and I had fun meeting new people while participating in an experience that gives back to the sport we both love. When the day came to do the race, I arrived ready to take on the task at hand with my friends Emmy and Janice, who had signed up to join me in taking turns pushing Jake. It was chilly, as it usually is in November in Wisconsin, and Jake was bundled up for his race. We had the opportunity to meet his family, and we had fun with Jake as we helped make his dream of finishing the race come true, even if it meant two hours of listening to the song "Shut Up and Dance" on repeat. The purpose for this run was very clear and completely outside any kind of performance goal for any of us. We were there for Jake, and it made the half-marathon feel like a breeze. The relief of knowing the why for each race intrigued me. I wanted this feeling to permeate my entire life, and I aimed to funnel all my decisions through an overall purpose, fueling it with passion. I knew this would be life changing for my athletes. I was able to make this a reality after much reflection and a solid dose of education post-Ironman 2017.

Now I believe my purpose is to inspire in all others the belief that anything is possible. I am here to educate and break down barriers.

Understanding this why paved the way to quickly and efficiently building on my foundation of honesty and worth through coaching, racing, and now writing. I have unearthed many explanations for the popular claim that racing is "mostly mental" and have focused on how to apply that understanding to *all* aspects of life. I have a strong desire to honor myself by understanding how each goal, small and large, serves my overall purpose. And I use my passions for endurance racing, for helping others, and for self-growth and loving well to keep my inner flame stoked. My feet feel firmly planted on the ground, and my foundation feels strong and unshakeable.

HOW YOU CAN LEARN FROM ME

- Determine a concrete reason for setting a goal—a why. Consider your overall life purpose and be willing to let it change in the flow of living. When it changes, take time to restructure your life in ways that honor the new why.
- Keep in mind that you have all the worthiness in you to achieve your goal, so don't focus on needing to prove anything to someone else or to yourself.
- Get to know yourself better to be more aware of the strengths and weaknesses of your character. Be aware when you decide to rely on excuses. Rise up against your personal reasons for not navigating life fully on your terms. Set goals for self-growth. Aim to actualize your full potential.
- Give back. Serving yourself doesn't mean being solely self-serving. Make adding value to the world part of your life's why.

DON'T LET COMPARISON IMPRISON

I coached under the umbrella of the Zone from 2011 until Kelli sold the gym in the spring of 2019. When the Zone became i2 Fitness, it was quickly clear they were not interested in a racing team or in-house coach. I had to decide if I would forge my own path again and become a new business owner. Kelli separated the triathlon team from the sale of the Zone, and we agreed to continue working together as co-owners of the Zone Racing Team. After personal reflection, I decided to continue my coaching career and created MB Coaching. MB not only stands for Miranda Bush but also, more importantly, *mind* over *body*. My business pays homage to the lesson I learned in my own training and coaching experience, which is that reaching your goal *is mostly a matter of mental strength, from conception to completion*. And by focusing on the goal, not lying to or distracting your mind, you have the opportunity to learn so much about navigating this one big life. I decided to combine health and race coaching to provide athletes with an experience I hope is truly life changing.

As I mentioned earlier, in the fall of 2019, I took a solo mission to Boulder, Colorado, to attend the TrainingPeaks Endurance Coaching Summit. I was slightly nervous, anticipating I would be a quiet learner at the conference rather than a contributing expert; however, I was ready to take my business to the next level by courageously going forth without the safety net of my family and friends. I had blurred professional and personal relations for a long time by training and coaching my close friends or becoming friends with the athletes over time, and so my clients knew my faults, mistakes, failures, and flaws. And although I had helped them and continued to guide them to great success, to many of them I was just Miranda—the imperfect, french fry–eating, beer-drinking, mistake-making mom of three. While I always want to be authentic and transparent, it is still hard to give athletes a constant front-row seat to my flaws. It was refreshing to go to Colorado and be mostly anonymous *Coach Miranda Bush*.

The urge to compare myself to others and immediately undermine my worthiness of attending this conference was strong at first—those imposter feelings are strong! It seemed that so many people knew each other in the industry, and all had the look of legit, professional coaches who, in my quick judgment, had most likely trained many high-performing athletes, maybe even Olympians, over the past several years.

In the opening lecture, we were told that we all had something to offer as experts in our profession. I remember this striking me as a new way to see myself. I had never considered myself an "expert" in anything, often because I would compare myself to someone who knew so much more or had been practicing their craft for much longer. I decided that I would consider myself an expert for the weekend's conference and bravely hold my head high, taking full advantage of the opportunities in front of me. I was quickly surprised to learn that most of my peers attending the conference were fairly new to their coaching careers also. At nearly every roundtable discussion, it was clear that we all had at least a foundational understanding of the basics of coaching: using software, periodization, general nutrition and hydration numbers, and data analysis. Again, I assessed through a healthy comparison where I stood with my peers. Most of the coaches attending were men, many of whom seemed to focus almost solely on numbers and metrics but struggled with getting their athletes to adhere to the plan. I did not commonly struggle with the same issues, so I was able to share my insights. I gave tips on assessing athlete readiness and the importance of seeing each client as an entire individual. I urged other coaches to look into their athletes' overall life to help them overcome hurdles so that they could consistently follow through in their training. We discussed having a strong reason, or why, for choosing to race. I suggested coaches take extra time on the front end to dig a little deeper into the psychology and readiness of training rather than end up "nagging" athletes on the back end.

When I spoke, I did so with authority, and the other coaches listened. I joined group runs in the mountains, not knowing how the altitude would affect my abilities, but I was able to share my story with fellow runners—albeit more out of breath than normal. I ran alongside and garnered the interest of one of the department heads of the leading coaching software companies with my ideas on new mental strategies. Because I had not let negative comparison kill my confidence, it opened the door to many more connections and opportunities.

I was not always able to step outside myself to see when comparison was ruling my thoughts and actions; however, going through the tough lessons of defining myself by the opinions of others was vital in learning and growing from it. When I opened the Zone in 2011, I had primarily been a stay-at-home mom for five years. I absolutely loved being home with my kids and am thankful for the ability to do so, but taking care of three kids, all one year apart, didn't provide for many accolades in the "workplace." So, when I opened the gym with the sincerest intention of helping people become their best selves, I was quickly drawn to the way the members built me up:

- "I want to look like you."
- "You are the best trainer I have ever had."
- "I love it here."
- "This gym is so much better than (insert gym name)."

The comparison lifted me up, and I built my worth as a trainer, instructor, and business owner on top of my shaky foundation of some self-awareness, a little pride, and a dash of insecurity. I was able to get up extremely early every day, not make one dollar, and carry the financial stress with the hope I could continue to help people and that they would continue to *like me*. In doing so, I fell into people-pleasing, which led me back to managing many different versions of myself in order to try to keep everyone happy, but my people-pleasing was selfishly driven. Eventually, I started to feel used up and could not offer myself fully to the members and the community. It was exhausting, very unproductive, and did not help me achieve my ultimate mission of guiding each individual to reach their goals. For a while, though, I was able to juggle the needs and wants of others while living silently in a suffering of my own making.

Over time I started to tire and could not keep up the facade. Then people began to see my imperfections, and sometimes they just didn't like me. At times their own insecurities led them to point out my flaws, and, when they struggled with achieving their goals due to their own hurdles, they would take the opportunity to tear me down. I could no longer keep everyone happy and started to accept that not everyone was going to like me, especially when I wasn't even giving them the chance to fully *know* the real me. I will never forget one statement from a member with whom I had worked a long time and whose goals I had. On a completely random day at the gym, as I was training for my Ironman 2013, she said, "I can't believe you are not skinnier with all the training you are doing." I was dumbfounded and embarrassed. I mumbled some kind of polite response, hurrying to get on with the workout, but this *stung.* I tried to bury the comment, but I remember catching a glimpse of my profile later when running past a storefront and many times in the mirror after that. This, combined with growing wisdom and awareness, started me on a crusade to change how I know, care about, and have compassion for myself. I did not want to be beholden to the opinions of others to validate my worth.

I had learned that comparison in the form of people-pleasing or aiming to validate your worth is unproductive and damaging.

Comparison based on insecurities often becomes a deflection for the real reasons your goals are not being met. These legitimate reasons can include a multitude of layered excuses and most likely have nothing to do with the other person or event. I have seen comparisons used as a cop out many times when priorities are not clear. I am also aware that we live in a society that capitalizes on comparison: *I will never be as good as them. Why even try?* *I will never look like that magazine cover. I might as well eat this packet of cookies.*

In the moment, we believe the deflection serves us better, allowing ourselves to believe the lie that we are better off not trying and heading down the path of least resistance. We believe this messaging from our culture is true. But the truth is, when working toward goals, there are two options—both with specific and unique challenges. One will encourage you to see where the messaging originates and find the tools to push through the resistance to get you closer to your stated goal. The other will keep creating resistance and obstacles through avoidance, leading you farther from your destination.

I don't see all comparisons as negative though. To prepare for success, we must use them to decide where we should start our journey. We can compare ourselves with other racers to have a clearer picture of how we will compete in the field. I have won three races in my life—one trail run, one Olympic-distance triathlon, and one ten-mile running race. The competitive field was very small for the tri and the running race, and I won both with lackluster effort. I won the trail run when the first-place woman took a wrong turn and ignored everyone's efforts to flag her down. Although I accepted my first-place trophy or medal, I used some healthy comparison to realistically evaluate my effort. I did win; yet I did not race at my best. So I got to tell people that I won the race while also knowing I couldn't continue putting in that lower amount of effort. I used comparison positively to assess my performance and decide to move forward with more vigor.

On the other hand, when we are motivated through negative comparison, we can take on the dark side of competitiveness, wishing that others would fail in order for us to have more success. We can decide we are not good enough for the challenge before we even start, giving us built-in excuses throughout the process and reasons we shouldn't even start at all. Oftentimes comparison can lead to judgment of others, too. When insecurities are high, we compare to feel better about ourselves. I see this as stepping on someone else's back to get to the top (and not in a cooperative way, like building a human pyramid, but in a shove-them-down way). Aggressive comparison that turns into uber-competitiveness or judgment will never work long term. It feeds on external motivation and ignores the emptiness within.

When you use comparison to seek out your "people," you must not become blind to the opportunities to form influential relationships with people whom you might see as different. This judgment is comparison that shuts doors on potentially exciting bonds. I have many friends who are different from me in terms of age, interests, style, ways of thinking, and so on. But I am thankful for the common bonds and shared values that have brought us together. If I focused on comparing myself to them from an outward standpoint, the opportunity to get to know them further would probably have passed me by. One beautiful friend is Annie, who knits me the warmest mittens to cover my constantly frozen hands in the Wisconsin winter. We have few interests in common but have a strong friendship through our faith, and we have prayed together and caught up every Tuesday for ten years. Then there's Janie, a spitfire of a woman older than my mother but a wonderfully inspiring friend. And Ted, a cool guy and ex-Marine who works a desk job whom I have had the honor to coach and befriend, and I was one of the first to know when he and his wife were expecting their son, Kyle. Also, Avery, a blinged-out gym-goer who always looks so put-together but comes to work her butt off and is funny, down to earth, and a joy to be around. Brenda is an energetic supermom, who is full of positivity and encouragement for others and gives me the gift of helping her find the same passion for herself. I could go on and on about the amazing people I have been fortunate to know through various avenues of my life. I don't knit, am not seventy years old, could never be a Marine or sit at a desk all day, never wear bling or often look put together, and I am no super mom; but if I had given into an initial comparison of myself to each of these amazing people, I would have lost the opportunities to build the friendships for which I am forever thankful.

HOW YOU CAN LEARN FROM ME

- Realize we all use comparison. Comparing can be useful at times, but don't be motivated by judgment.
- Believe in your worthiness. Align yourself appropriately with your competitors at the start line, but don't decide then, or in the process, that you are not good enough to be there. You are worthy of whatever realistic goal you decide to tackle.
- Keep in mind that comparison can also seep into potential relationships. Don't decide that someone "isn't for you" without giving them a chance.
- Seek to understand. When you have opportunities to learn rather than compare, take them!

HONOR YOUR NEEDS (AND WANTS)

In the late fall of 2006, after deciding I would take on a future Ironman, I signed up for my first ever race—a half-marathon in the following April. Yes, I decided to take on 13.1 miles instead of doing what I would suggest all my athletes do—start with a 5K. But I didn't believe I needed permission from anyone to take this on as my first race. So I signed up. Jamie surprised me with a pair of new running tights and an iPod, and I printed off one of the beginner's running plans by the legendary Hal Higdon. I followed the plan exactly as written, often running my longer runs at 4:30 a.m. I arrived at the start line completely solo and very uneducated about racing. But I was so excited. It ended up being a great race, and I ran my half-marathon PR, which held up for several years of racing the distance.

I am very thankful for a central belief that started from a very young age: I don't need permission to make choices to live my life as I please. I took this idea a little (or a lot) too far when I was young, leaning way too much toward selfishness and narcissism. Though my pendulum swung away from this destructive youthful thinking, thankfully the core of this message remained. If I had an inkling to take on a goal, whether it was to move heavy furniture while nine months pregnant or taking on a big race, I didn't need to ask permission.

As with many modeled behaviors, we often learn as we get older and wiser that some of these ideas could benefit from being refined. I still don't ask permission from society at large to go after what I want, but I do consider the impact on my family, friends, other priorities, community, humanity, and my overall well-being. I try to thoughtfully consider decisions, more of a dialogue and less of a dictatorship within my own mind. When it comes to setting race goals, I have learned the importance of listening to my inner voice so that I can make a clear assessment of the strength of the desire and the purpose for it. If it is strong, I talk it through with Jamie and articulate why it is important to me. He is a supportive husband who champions my dreams, so this most often ends up being enough for me to pursue my goal. But this is not because he is *letting* me; he is *supporting* me. I try to not use manipulation, but sometimes my desire to control situations and/or people overcomes what I know to be "the right thing." I communicate my sincere desire to participate in each race.

I now know that my raw ignorance kept me from running even better both in training and on race day at my first race in April 2007. Nevertheless, I am thrilled I decided that I wanted something and had the courage to listen to the nudge and take on the challenge. Too often we judge even the desire for such goals. We have so many obstacles that can pop up along the way, some from our own past experiences or learned behavior from family of origin or other upbringing influence. Much of our decision-making is clouded by cultural messaging and marketing influences. You don't need permission to make the decision to live your most authentic life. I suggest choosing a goal that serves your purpose, having a why for taking it on, and (mostly) knowing that you will not intentionally harm family, friends, or any other member of the human race. But you obviously don't need my permission either.

Trust your thinking and take on the challenge.

To stop asking permission, we need to practice trusting ourselves. And, in order to trust yourself, you have to *be you*. Write your "who I am" statement. Seek to understand the things you enjoy. Honor your wants and needs. It is not selfish to know what you need and go for it first; it is only selfish when doing so comes at the expense of others. Be aware so that you know the difference and act out of care for yourself and others. Make decisions and stick to them. Push yourself out of your comfort zone. Give yourself time and patience to grow. Learn to manage and be more realistic with expectations. Be honest, not only with others but with *yourself.*

The foundational work of building self-awareness through mindfulness leads to a better understanding of ourselves and, hopefully, more trust. I practice this in myself by making some concrete decisions about many things weekly without enlisting the input of anyone else. (I also do have mentors and teachers, but I dedicated a whole part of this book to that topic). I suggest that, if you have a lack of trust in yourself, you should aim to know yourself on a deeper level: spend some quiet time alone, ask yourself what you need and want, visualize these things coming true, and then use your moral compass to make the decisions that you want to make, without asking permission.

A big part of honoring your needs and wants is knowing when to pivot. 2020 could be known as the year of the pivot, whether we wanted to face the circumstances or not. Luckily, I had done a fair amount of work connecting to my wants and needs, regardless of the events of the pandemic that were clearly far out of my control. I had to support my husband as he pivoted trying to figure out how to maintain our restaurant businesses. Kelli and I had to make constant pivots on our race team plans, while trying to motivate and encourage members when races were canceled and spirits were low. I had to pivot from my normal spring and summer of building up fitness to take on huge race goals, a schedule that typically also filled many of my social needs.

I feel like 2020 was the story of pivot, pivot, pivot in constant circles.

But we became more resilient and learned to make the most of the uncertainty. I kept training, and, after it was clear that all races were going to be canceled (post-lockdown), I took on a solo race distance challenge from my coach. Four distances in one month, one each week. I defined my why for each "race" and enjoyed time with friends and my newfound training partner, my husband. Rather than stand in one place, too afraid to fall, I embraced this pivot. I completed a super sprint with my friend Kelli, a sprint with a group of girlfriends, and an Olympic with my daughter Halle and Jamie. I finished the challenge with a 70.3 on a sweltering Tuesday, in my small town, swimming in the pool, biking with Jamie, and running alone. It was hard, but I am thankful I did it. When racing opened up again, I excitedly aimed my training toward Chattanooga 70.3, slated for May 2021. I was faced with another choice to pivot when my kids' prom was scheduled, and thankfully I was able to sign up for Ironman Texas 70.3 in Lubbock, which ended up being quite the adventure and learning opportunity.

Our trip to Lubbock started off with some rough travel. We had plane issues on both flights that led to longer times sitting in a cramped seat, the stress of almost missing our connection, missing luggage, and nutrition and sleep disruptions. Traveling by air to a race was a relatively new experience for me, so I tried to take it in my stride and learn how to plan better for the future. The forecast had changed from one-hundred-plus degrees and sun to seventy-five degrees and storms. I didn't dwell on it and followed my own advice of not obsessively checking the weather. There wasn't much time or energy for course reconnaissance, so on race morning, I showed up ready to go. I stupidly chose to swim without a wet suit, even though it was declared "wet suit legal," and I am not a strong enough swimmer to compete well without my wet suit. The swim was murky and rough, and I never got into a good rhythm. I came out of the water disappointed, my teeth visibly chattering. I worked to warm up and accept my swim time while out on the bike and was in good spirits on the ride, even though the course, with its smooth roads, was boring as hell.

When I got off the bike ready to run, I hadn't seen Jamie since the start of the bike leg, but we had discussed him potentially not seeing me at many spots on the bike, due to the difficulty presented for spectators navigating an out-and-back course. When I exited the bike to run transition (T2), I anticipated seeing his smiling face. The run was three loops through the Texas Tech campus, with loads of spectators. I smiled and scanned the crowd. Still no Jamie. As I came around each corner, I would think, *I know I will see him now*, and when I didn't, I started to slide into the *what-ifs*. By the time I completed the first loop, I was filled with worry and dread. My husband is reliable and resourceful, and he never gets lost. I became convinced something was very wrong, and with only the two of us in Texas together, I started to panic.

At mile six, I needed to call him. I flagged down an EMT, who let me use his phone. I cannot describe the relief I felt when Jamie answered. It turns out he was stuck in a ditch. The rain had washed out a road, and what had looked like gravel was Texas clay. He told me to keep running. As I took off, the EMT yelled, "He says he loves you." I was relieved yet suddenly exhausted. The heightened emotional response of dread followed by the strong relief created a new challenge for me. I ran the rest of the race in a constant mental battle of *This place and race is cursed. Just walk to the finish*, and *This is an opportunity to use your tools. Keep fighting.*

When I finished, I was happy, but it also felt weird. I have never finished a big race completely alone. I felt disappointment in my time, yet I was sincerely proud I never gave up. I won the mental battle in the end, even if my time and placement wasn't what I knew I was capable of. I looked around and considered all the reasons I race. I talked to some strangers and smiled. I felt all the feels.

At least, I did in that moment. In case you were not aware, racing a half-Ironman is exhausting, and the hurdles didn't stop presenting themselves at the end of the race. Some were out of my control, and some were very much put up by me. And as they kept popping up, I felt less and less capable of jumping over them. On the way home, we sat on the plane for hours before leaving Lubbock and missed our connection in Dallas. We caught a flight to Minneapolis and scrambled to find a way home from Minnesota. It was defeating and emotionally, physically, mentally, and financially exhausting. By the time I got home, I felt heavy with disappointment and frustration. And I didn't handle it well. After several of my meltdowns, Jamie demanded that I stop being snarky and mean. In an effort not to feel the full weight of my letdown and disappointment over my failed race goal, I had tried to move very quickly past it, and in just hours post-race, I entered the realm of *toxic positivity*.

Toxic positivity is the belief that no matter how dire or difficult a situation, people should maintain a positive mindset—a "good vibes only" approach to life. I had wanted *only* good vibes while having some alone time with my husband in Texas. My toxic positivity was my way of holding it together during our journey home and for the days after, waiting a week to receive my mislaid bike and luggage. While I value a positive mindset, I preach against toxic positivity because I aim to live an honest, full, and real life, which involves a lot of negative emotion. I sincerely aim to connect to my body, allowing myself to feel negative and positive feelings. But I am human. And when not operating with a focused mind and aware heart, we all have our go-to defense against negative emotion. Some buffer with alcohol, food, social media, or keeping busy, while others prefer to blame others, becoming the victim. My default buffer is to quickly put on the rose-colored glasses in an effort to not feel the pain and hurt that comes with negativity. Instead of curiously inspecting how

I am feeling, I try to forcibly manipulate my brain into not feeling the negative emotion.

I am blessed! I am thankful! I am going to learn so much from this failure!

After my race in Texas, that pain was in the form of disappointment. I only allowed myself to feel it for a very short time, quickly moving on to focusing on gratitude and lessons learned. While I believe in expressing gratitude, I also know the vital importance of fully feeling through the negative emotion. My pre-race strategy was derailed, so my post-race recovery pretty much sucked, worsened by poor sleep, no food for hours, long travel, and the stress of missing luggage. And upon our return, life didn't halt to give me a second to breathe. I am a mom and have a job. I kept trying to smile and be positive, to push my real feelings to the back of my mind in order to give the best version of me. Guess what? This didn't work for long. It took four days of fighting it and having it come out sideways for it to basically take me down. I cried. I let myself fully feel it. And guess what? I felt much better. I felt honest. I learned that my husband and friends still love me. They love the *real* me.

I needed to learn these lessons so that I could stop acting selfishly when I couldn't pretend that "everything is awesome" anymore. I needed to trust myself, my family, and my friends to honor my real feelings and that they would give me the space to feel through them with kindness and compassion. I needed to *feel* so that I could look at my efforts, goals, joys, and failures with honesty. I needed to be faced with the challenges in order to grow; I didn't want to strive for easy or comfortable. I wanted to feel it all. The chance of pain is worth the opportunity for joy. It is all part of a real and full life.

I had learned (and relearned) some very important lessons for my next race and also for understanding my athletes better. But I didn't know how quickly I would need to apply those lessons. In the late summer of 2021, we prepared for another tornado of emotion when Halle went off to college. She chose to go to the University of Wisconsin, close to home, but as a driven, independent young woman, who had much of her high school experience altered from the pandemic, we knew she was ready to leave home. I knew I would miss her, but I was sincerely excited to see her spread her wings.

Halle and I have always had a very open relationship, and no topics were off-limits in discussion with my kids as they grew up. She desires to see us often, and that fills my heart with sincere joy. But when she inevitably started to share the details of her college social life, I hit a breaking point. I did, yet didn't, want to know that she was making choices I did not agree with. Although she is becoming an adult, I still see her as my little girl. And after some time and space, I realized I hadn't allowed myself to feel through the shifting in our relationship. Our family had been affected by some awful trauma, and rather than focus on grieving and accepting the fact my oldest child and only daughter is moving on, I made the mistake of feigning "perspective" by comparing my hurt to that of others and ignoring the need. Finally, I allowed myself to feel the change, and now I am more intentional about loving her and myself as we are *right now*.

Being able to feel and pivot when needed without anger or guilt is a way of honoring your needs and wants. But first you have to establish a mindset built on the truth that you do not have to be a constant victim of circumstances. Unfortunately, we live in a society that loves to place blame on others. This oddly feels comforting in the moment, but in reality, it gives your power to someone or something else. When we are stuck under the control and influence of other things, it is hard to confidently pivot because we often lack trust in our own decision-making. Not only are we constantly inundated with conflicting and confusing messages from outside sources, but we are also afraid that if we take full ownership and change direction we might disappoint others—we might disappoint ourselves.

I have been inspired to pivot many times by some very influential people in my life, including athletes who show up to each race ready to tackle their goal, no matter the size of the waves or the weather— like my friend Joe, a talented triathlete who consistently and confidently shows up at races and conquers massive goals. I am also in awe of athletes who experienced physical trauma that forced them to decide between giving in or pivoting to take on challenging goals via parasport. Or professional athletes, musicians, and artists who choose to overcome difficult circumstances to be the best at their craft. They had to make a decision to pivot and harness their new norm as power for their own life goals.

I have seen this firsthand for almost twenty-two years in my husband, Jamie. He faced much adversity in his upbringing that impacted his ability to easily honor his own needs and wants. In the past, he had always put the needs of others before his own, even if he felt resentful or unhappy doing so. But recently, facing some tough times and hurdles in his professional life, I have had the honor of watching him pivot toward self-care and respect. He has shown grace and forgiveness for himself. He no longer makes reluctant and erratic pivots, motivated by stress and stubbornness, and now changes his direction to care more for his needs. It is exciting, endearing, motivating, and inspiring.

HOW YOU CAN LEARN FROM ME

- Cultivate self-awareness. In order to know what you want and need, you must practice getting to know you.

- Communicate when setting big goals. After determining your desires, discuss them confidently with the people who will be most affected—often your family and close friends. Before presenting your case, consider the following question: Will my decision to take on this goal harm anyone? Enter these conversations with an open mind and heart, but be prepared to honor your needs.

- Trust yourself. Spend some time alone so that you understand yourself better and are able to hear the inner voice of intuition. Make concrete decisions about small things and then bigger ones. This will not be as easy as flipping a switch, but it can get better with practice. Like all things, seek a professional, if needed.

- Be mindful of your desire to take on toxic positivity. Don't drown your real feelings. Allow yourself to experience negative emotion.

- Learn to pivot from a place of trust and awareness of your own needs. Don't quit on yourself, but don't be completely rigid with goals. Life changes. Focus on what you can control after acknowledging your emotions and allowing yourself to feel them.

PART 3

DARE TOGETHER

No road is long with good company.
TURKISH PROVERB

TAKE CARE OF YOURSELF TO BETTER CARE FOR OTHERS

In 2018 I was still managing group exercise at Zone Fitness and Training. I decided to launch a New Year program called Find and Fuel Your Passion. This was born out of the realization that members were not missing the opportunities to reach goals through lack of desire, but for a multitude of other reasons. For this program, I planned to offer tools to help them dig deeper into themselves and learn about the real purpose for these goals. I was ready to share my messages of the importance of knowing yourself and establishing and believing in a solid why. Other central themes of this program included learning how to recognize cultural lies, stop leaning toward martyrdom, and learning more about self-worth. I had to teach them how to care for themselves first. We didn't discuss bubble baths and pedicures, but the nitty-gritty of what self-care really means and why it is integral to actualizing your full potential.

To *care* for yourself is to put your needs first so that you are better able to serve others. It took some time to convince the program participants that caring for yourself is not selfish but the opposite. Selfishness is caring for yourself at the *expense* of others. I persuaded them that they needed to practice self-love in order to build efficacy, confidence, and esteem. These building blocks would provide them with the tools to confidently move forward in goal actualization.

Early on in my marriage, I learned about setting boundaries. Not only do they help create stronger and healthier relationships, but setting boundaries is one of the biggest forms of self-love. Establishing and holding boundaries allows you to focus on being proactive on your needs rather than reactive. I had blurred boundaries many times over the years through codependency and my intense need to please people. Trying to change rather than understand people in toxic friendships had taken over my time and my heart. I didn't know myself well, and without boundaries I was unable to turn away from things that felt good and exciting in the moment to do what I needed to do to stay strong, centered, and moving forward in my life. I had to learn what I needed and then stay focused on it, turning away from automatic behavior patterns that kept me making the same mistakes of my past. I needed *boundaries*. Boundaries are not walls but fences—the kind you can see through and that often have gates only controlled by the owner. They are established to meet your needs so that you can in turn practice more kindness to others. Just as a fence establishes the outline of your property, boundaries set the basic guidelines on how

you want to be treated. They are a form of self-care and self-respect.
Setting and maintaining boundaries is a foundational part of having healthy relationships and being able to give back to others.

Boundaries are also important in parenting. My oldest and middle children are six days short of a year apart. And there are only fourteen months between my second and third child. My early twenties were very busy with making, having, and nursing babies. My biggest challenges, joys, and daily lessons have been through my role as a *mom.* Even now, I have been told by many that *I have my hands very full.* And like all parents, I still do, even though my "kids" are now young adults. I love my kids unconditionally and would sacrifice my own life for them at any time if faced with that decision. But as we all exist on this earth together, I will not give up who I am in the name of loving them more. I refuse to let go of boundaries and love them as a martyr parent. Author Glennon Doyle defines *martyr parenting* perfectly in her book *Untamed*:

> We (mothers) have lived as if she who disappears the most, loves the most. We have been conditioned to pour out our love by slowly ceasing to exist.
>
> These lessons resonated with me and put me on a path of loving my children while still honoring myself. I will not cease to exist. I will not be a model of disappearing out of love.
>
> I will do things to honor myself.

I have been a mom through my entire triathlon career. Each one of us has our individual journeys, but I am empathetic through my own experience as well as compassionate through my extensive research on the pressures that moms face in sport and beyond. Although the lack of establishing boundaries and martyr parenting does fall on the parent, Doyle also reminds us how we have been conditioned by our culture.

"Mom guilt" refers to the specific feelings of guilt mothers experience that relate to their role as a mother and their ability to meet their child(ren)'s needs. As I mentioned, I suffered from mom guilt early on in my parenting life. I was not and am not alone. Overcoming mom guilt is one of the biggest obstacles to us taking time daily for ourselves, whether it is to train for races, or any other hobby, work, etc. This is most definitely a big-picture problem, one that takes a shift in cultural ideas bigger than any individual can do in the flip of a switch. But, I do believe that we can work toward change, starting with gaining a greater understanding of these pressures.

"Good," or "loving" mothers are often portrayed as being *constantly* attentive, present, and patient. This standard is completely unrealistic, often leaving moms feeling guilty for real human feelings like boredom, anger, resentment, annoyance, exhaustion, the desire to have space from the responsibility and/or stress of parenting, or simply the interest in doing something else. Those of us who want to work will obviously fall short in the "attentive" and "constantly present" expectations. And if we choose a recreational hobby, time with friends, or travel (to name just a few other things moms might want to do), we often feel the pressure to justify our decisions to electively spend any amount of time away from our kid(s).

I was fortunate to have a friend and mentor in Kylie to help me renounce mom guilt. Now, as I mentioned, my "kids" have now all moved out to attend college. I have often had a hard time navigating this transitional season of life, but I accept that they are moving on to be themselves. They are confident. They are strong. I believe that through goal setting and establishing boundaries I have modeled that real love is honoring yourself and connecting with others who love themselves as well. I hope I have shown them self-respect and self-care. I have loved them even when they have made mistakes—and they haven't made nearly as many as I did as a teen or young adult.

Honoring my needs allows me to truly follow and trust my passions. I have not had to hide behind anyone, especially not my kids. I continue to go after big goals and make them a priority in my daily life because I have chosen to be a role model rather than a martyr, to be in the driving seat of my own life rather than being a passenger. Kids will continue to take all you are willing to give, but even if they seemingly want everything from you in the present moment, they do not want to grow up believing they are the reason you didn't live as you. That is too great a burden to bear.

By establishing boundaries and modeling a life of continual growth and awareness, my family has been able to maintain pretty solid relationships. I feel no resentment for spending years investing in them. We have fun together and race together. Halle can lap me in the pool (several times) and always beats me out of the water in a race. Deaken beat me overall in a race for the first time in 2019 and will continue to crush me whenever he races. Quinton always smashes me on the run. They try their best, and I am extremely proud of them. But I don't claim their wins as my own, nor do I remind them of all the sacrifices I had to make to be their mom. We race together as *teammates*.

Taking care of yourself includes accepting and living well in your physical body. I weigh myself roughly twice a year (at my coach's request for sweat-rate test data). I coach people on loving their bodies as they are in any given moment rather than putting any amount of importance on a number. I realized long ago that I would often weigh myself when I was feeling good—good about how I physically looked and felt. But if the number on the scale wasn't where I thought it should be, I would end up feeling sad and disappointed. And in that moment, the single thing that changed my feeling was a number I didn't like. Now, when I feel good, I just allow myself to feel good; I don't need the validation of the scale.

I post often on social media with the intent of reaching others with my message, which has given me the opportunity to reflect on validation outside the number on the scale. The social media game is a constant barometer on how much I am seeking outward validation. Some days I post a picture or a reel and check back endlessly to see if people "like" it. Other days I ignore it other than to check comments, putting no ownership on the external. When I am feeling more self-aware, I can reflect on my reaction to the feedback of friends and strangers. And when I am not, it impacts me positively and/or negatively until I become more aware. I know that the heart of my message is to reach more people in order to inspire and encourage. So I do try to post my authentic self—in anything from sweatshirts and joggers to swimsuits and sports bras.

I have had the honor of coaching women and men of many different sizes and shapes. Fortunately, although I am not immune to diet culture messaging, I have not personally struggled with disordered eating, body dysmorphia, or obesity. When I was new to my fitness career, many women would come to me saying they want a body "like mine." I would assume they meant they wanted to be physically and mentally strong and healthy, but over time I realized they were approaching this way of thinking more literally than I imagined—they wanted to actually *look like me*. Maybe they didn't want short brown hair, brown eyes, and a bit of a crooked smile, but they wanted a body shape similar to mine. Most often they were not five feet nine inches and had completely different body types. At first it was flattering, but after unearthing how much of a negative impact that diet culture had on their self-worth, it made me want to further my mission to speak truth to people about loving their bodies.

Nancy, an ex-client, was one of the first people to show me the impact of how such a pervasive diet culture can breed insecurities in women. *Diet culture* is defined in many ways. Simply put, it is the pervasive belief that appearance and body shape are more important than physical, psychological, and general well-being. As a new trainer, I was and still am thankful for the opportunities that Nancy gave me to apply my knowledge, but she also taught me how to notice when someone is projecting their own insecurities onto you. We became friends, and I sincerely liked Nancy. She has qualities that are endearing, and she is worthy of love and friendship. But she didn't know her worthiness at the time and could frankly be quite mean at times. Nancy is almost ten years older than me, and we have completely different body types, but she consistently wanted to compare herself to me. When she was feeling good about herself, she would compliment me, give me gifts, and refer clients to work with me. But when she didn't like something, rather than come to me, she would complain to others and tear me down, not only professionally but personally. She would comment on my appearance and weight often, again depending on her mood. I eventually had to establish some pretty strong boundaries.

I could spend many chapters on defining *diet culture*, sharing stories on how much impact it has had on myself and others, and how much I truly hate the hold it takes on women. The best thing I have done for myself is to inform and educate myself and others, to try to see the lies it tells us, and to rid my social media feed and other sources of mental uptake of unhealthy ways of approaching food or appearance. It is a powerful machine and will continue to infiltrate our spaces, but I do believe in our power to continue to fight back for change. After stepping away from a relationship with Nancy, I see how she was under the gross spell of diet culture. I understand the guiding force behind her emotions and treatment of me, and I am not angry with her, but even more fueled in my message to end this way of negatively viewing and judging our physical bodies. It is ultimately what led me away from a career in personal training, where most of my clients were interested in weight-loss goals, and instead toward a celebration of what our bodies can do in endurance sports.

HOW YOU CAN LEARN FROM ME

- Love yourself to love your kids (and all others). You, your relationships, and humanity will benefit.
- Practice intentional self-care. In addition to spiritually, emotionally, and mentally, take care of your basic needs. Nourish yourself daily through movement, nutritious foods, proper sleep, physical connection, and healthy social interactions.
- Establish and uphold boundaries. Honor both yourself and others by being clear and consistent.
- Reflect on what you think a "good" mom is. Write these traits down. Inspect them for truth while considering how your upbringing and ingested societal norms helped shape your expectations. Decide which thought patterns you can change.
- Stop judging the actions of others, including moms. Consider your language around societal norms surrounding parenting. Don't ask leading or loaded questions.
- Don't decide that moms can only have space because they "need it." Moms *deserve* to do what they need because they are worthy of it, not because they earned it through endless sleepless nights, a million temper tantrums, or weeks spent planning a Pinterest-worthy birthday party.

- Support and/or help a mom. Offer to watch their kids so they can train, race, or enjoy spending their time however they want to away from their kids. Ask about their work and hobbies as much as you ask about their family. Like and comment on their personal endeavors that they share on social media as much as you do for posts of their kids' activities and accomplishments.
- Educate yourself on our culture's messaging surrounding martyr parenting, mom guilt, and diet culture. You can fight back against the things that are seemingly out of our outward control while simultaneously finding ways to live better in this present world.

NURTURE RELATIONSHIPS AND JOIN COMMUNITIES

It may be tempting to think that we would have the best chance at peace by spending every minute of our lives figuring out our own brains. But as humans, we were never meant to be solitary. While it is vital we cultivate a mindful approach to our lives in order to best serve others, we must then go out and build relationships and serve our community. At times this is simple; at other times it's very hard. It sometimes means interacting with people who we believe we understand. Other times people appear to be absolutely impossible. The true joy of life comes in learning to see all people as doing the best we can. We connect best by giving back, enjoying other people, and putting aside our privilege to learn more from relationships and communities.

As I have mentioned, I co-own a local race team with my good friend Kelli. And if I may say so, our team is unbelievably awesome.

I believe one of the most important ways that endurance sports serve us is through connection to each other through a common goal. Camaraderie includes a trust that everyone is showing up for a combination of similar reasons—out of a love for the sport(s); a desire to challenge oneself; and/or a need for a daily exercise training habit, to name just a few. Our team shows up to connect with and support each other, and I have been more than blessed to have so many people come into my life through Zone Racing. Connecting with people is an essential part of living a full life.

We are not meant to live alone, especially not a life of passion. I wholly believe in kindness and the value of putting ourselves among strangers. I also believe romantic and/or platonic relationships are mutually beneficial for growth. Maybe you have seen memes floating around social media that tell us it is better to have a small number of close friends than a lot of acquaintances or followers; however, this advice is one-dimensional and not completely true. We need it all. The tight bonds and the broad communities. From the spouse who will bicker with you during a race and still hug you at the end to the spectators lining the paths and streets clanging cowbells, everyone is important in some way. The people we choose to spend time with reflect our own values and character, and these people influence our thoughts and actions. I have learned that spending most of my time with healthy and supportive—*but not perfect*—people is integral to living with passion.

In addition to our team, my core community of immediate family— now including spouses, nieces, and nephews—have supported me in my physical endeavors. What I have learned from these relationships has allowed me to not only improve these relationships themselves but also to better my own familial and overall roles. They have taught and continue to teach me about the importance of understanding, cooperation, and unconditional love. My grandparents all modeled hard work, love, and acceptance, and this trickled down to my fabulous aunts, uncles, and cousins. My extended family, and many of Jamie's, continue to shape and guide the person I am today by showing up and sharing hardship, joy, and inspiration. He and I have received so much support for all our endeavors, from raising our family to establishing businesses to reaching personal goals. I once even had a fellow racer say to me during Ironman Wisconsin in 2013, "Are you Miranda? You are like a celebrity out here!"

My first triathlon team, APG, was full of amazing people and helpful mentors who were fun to talk to and celebrate success with. The congregation and pastor of my first church, Point of Grace, and my wonderful friend Sandy, who introduced me to the church, provided a safe place for me to learn and grow in my relationship with God. Our friends Leslie and Jess and Chloe and Chuck taught us the value of traveling with other adults in order to have some freedom from the daily responsibilities of work and raising kids, as well as the fun that comes with anticipating surprises.

These individuals and collective communities heavily influence my life. The women and men of the Zone still add much value and inspiration. I have so many friends whom I met through the kids' sports, but have become like family. I admire Ava and Reese for their openness and loving hearts; Mauve for her willingness to go above and beyond for friends; Belinda for her driven spirit and willingness to allow everyone their own journey; Gini for her fun-loving ease with friends (and her fiery spirit); Winnie for her strength in growth and vulnerability in sharing; Fiona for her passion and willingness to learn and do hard things; Deb for her encouraging spirit; and so many more for their fun companionship. My friend Annie, who couldn't be any less like me but is a sister of faith who prays with me weekly, puts up with my constant life drama and knits me the warmest mittens I have ever owned. I have celebrated the joy of life with many friends through so many years—I could never name them all.

My friendships with many men are also vital to my life and growth, among them Marc, Aaron, Mitch, Ron, Blake, and Mark. I also highly value the relationships with the youth of our team, especially Grace, Emma, and Brooke, whom I have had the blessed experience of coaching and seeing become young adults. And I am forever blessed and grateful for the adults and children of our "framily," the close-knit, influential adult friendships mentioned throughout, but also including the kids: Abby, Quinn, Odin, Piper, Willah, Avery, Joey, and Emme.

I had to learn the importance of understanding, respecting, and honoring myself so that I could find "my people." It has helped me live with a clearer understanding of shared or conflicting values and where I can establish healthy boundaries. I see the value of cultivating relationships that are not codependent but interdependent. I have focused on trying to stop taking the actions of others so personally. I know now that I benefit from nurturing relationships with people who I can truly be myself with, share my realness with, wrestle through hard stuff with, and count on to listen with open hearts. These relationships are worth examining when there are emotional red flags or strain. These are the people who encourage and support my growth. These are *interdependent* relationships.

Interdependent relationships are when two strong individuals are involved with each other without sacrificing themselves or compromising their values. These relationships can be romantic, friendly, or familial, in which each person values their own identity and can fully be themselves. These close relationships are not perfect, or without conflict. But in them both people feel like they can be their whole selves. The relationship adds value to our lives. Both people find time for personal interests and other important relationships.

Some positive characteristics of interdependent relationships include enjoying clear, consistent communication; taking personal responsibility for one's actions within the relationship; respecting each other's boundaries; listening with empathy but without needing to fix the other's problems; expressing vulnerability together while still feeling safe; and raising each other's self-esteem. And when values, priorities, or proximity shift, both parties can pivot within or out of the relationship with grace and love.

Unhealthy romantic relationships or friendships are often classified as "codependent." The term itself sounds kind of cozy, *but it is not*. Some red flags that might signal codependency include people-pleasing, lack of establishing boundaries, poor self-esteem, reacting rather than acting with intentionality, an unhealthy dependence on each other, and relationship stress. Codependency stifles the growth of each individual. This kind of relationship enables unhealthy behaviors in both parties rather than breeding real support. Luckily, you can overcome codependency to create *inter*dependence. We can do this by separating *support* from codependency. Healthy support, rather than unhealthy enabling, includes offering compassion and acceptance, talking and listening, and discussing possible solutions but stepping back to allow each party to make their own decisions.

We all know relationships take work. But keep in mind that "work" is not innately bad; it just means that relationships, especially the deepest ones, cannot exist on autopilot. They take effort from both individuals. Therefore, it is not always true that "easy" relationships are the ones that are *meant to be*. I often think of a message from Mitchell, a previous pastor of mine. In a message years ago, he said, "You know that a relationship matters when you experience real conflict and can work through it with honesty, trust, forgiveness, and grace—when you can come out on the other side with more understanding than before." Some nurturing practices he shared with me include listening with empathy without trying to fix problems for the other person, practicing polite refusals, and considering how your actions will affect you and your energy.

No one is perfect; therefore no one can be perfect for each other. The relationships that are worth working on are the ones in which you can each be yourselves, be honest and forgiving, establish healthy boundaries, practice empathetic listening, and align your respective values in a mutually respectful way. They are not always happy or simple, but they should not create or enable toxicity. Healthy relationships allow individuals' passions to flourish and add value to each person's life in clear ways that you don't have to dig for, search for, or justify. These relationships energize and inspire you to give to your communities and close friends and family. They inspire you to be the best you.

It is also true that, as I have always told my kids, you don't have to *like* everyone, but you have to *be kind*. When we understand boundaries and have healthy friendships, we can navigate life easier with acquaintances and strangers. It will become less about right versus wrong or good versus bad people. We can live with a sense of peace, trusting that we are all out here doing the best we can.

Most of the time, the actions of others are rarely about you anyway.

I have learned much from relationships. I have experienced codependency and dependency. I have felt the confusion of being lured into relationships with codependency as the goal. I have people-pleased. I have been a wife, mother, and friend with a strong sense of self; and I have been an insecure wife, mom, and friend with low self-esteem. I am not perfect and will never strive to be. I have, however, been intent on leaning into learning, not striving but remaining curious about myself and others.

HOW YOU CAN LEARN FROM ME

- Evaluate your relationships—not under a microscope of judgment, but from a place of desiring deeper understanding. Keep in mind that no one, including you, is perfect.
- Aim to create and nurture close interdependent romantic relationships and friendships. Look to understand each other. Talk about how your values align. Do not get yourself into a "need" situation with relationships, but instead focus on a deeper and more meaningful "want."
- Join communities. Spend time with people who have common interests and learn more about the individuals. Be open to new friendships. Spend time with different kinds of people. Learn from the ones who don't like you and/or are different from you.
- Serve with your heart. Love yourself and others hard. Follow your dreams. Live with passion.

CELEBRATE IMPORTANT FRIENDSHIPS

It is such a gift in a world influenced by the notion that women are "catty" and insincere to have female friends who help bring out the best in you with their honesty and shared desire to grow. My good friend Molly has been essential in my story. I met Molly in the early spring of 2009. We had just moved to Oregon, Wisconsin, from nearby

Madison. That morning, with a stocking hat masking my bed head, I had pulled on whatever boots I had found lying around over my pajama pants. And when I met fully made-up Molly at the bus stop, I immediately wondered if we could be friends. She was the vision of "put-together"; I was the vision of "falling apart." But she was friendly and introduced herself and the other moms, and said hello to my daughter, Halle, who was starting a new school midway through her kindergarten year. Later, Molly learned that my youngest, Quinton, was only two weeks younger than her son, Quinn. She invited him over for a playdate, and soon our whole families connected. Molly and I shared many values and ideas, especially surrounding parenting. In 2009 I was preparing for my first Ironman and had been teaching group exercise for a little over a year at a couple of local gyms. That summer I offered to hold a small free boot camp in the park for some of the neighbor friends, including Molly. After that, some of the women joined one of the local gyms I had started teaching at, Harmony Zone Fitness. Roughly a year later, Molly, who had been a Harmony Zone member since the previous fall, came to me with a short list scratched on a piece of paper. She had decided that I had the capability to venture into my own fitness business. She had done research and had found a location and offered her help.

Her raw belief in me and willingness to share it was a life-changing catalyst, encouraging me to consider my own capabilities in a new and exciting way.

As we considered the options over the next couple of months, I was made aware that the two women who owned Harmony Zone Fitness were planning to sell the gym. The timing aligned perfectly with my youngest child going to kindergarten, thereby ending my need to be a mostly full-time stay-at-home parent. Molly and Jamie fully supported and encouraged me to buy the gym. I was confident

I could be a valued trainer and instructor, but I was very unsure of the business side, so Molly offered to work for me, using her previous experience in office management. After many negotiations, I found out in November 2010, while on vacation in Mexico with Jamie, that I would be a new gym owner as of the end of December.

Molly and I got to work immediately upon my return preparing to open Zone Fitness and Training on January 2, 2011. We set up an LLC, designed a logo, and tackled many other new-business tasks. We also got started on our version of the existing New Year accountability program, Happy (and Healthy) New You. Our preparation was going well, and we were both excited to take on the new venture.

Early in the morning of December 5, 2010, things were upended. I was traveling my normal route to Gold's Gym in a neighboring community to teach one of my last 5:30 a.m. group boot camp classes. As I neared an intersection, I saw a car turn left erratically onto the road I was traveling, headlights coming directly at me. I swerved to avoid a head-on collision, and she swerved as well, in the same direction, maintaining our unintended game of chicken. I realized there was a very good chance I was going to have my first car accident as I swerved one more time to avoid her and ended up taking out a fence, hitting a tree, and being hit in the back by the driver as she zoomed by, leaving the accident scene. I don't remember losing consciousness, but I do recall finding my phone to dial 911. As I talked with the dispatcher, a couple appeared at my passenger-side door to see if I was okay. I assumed they had been in the car that hit me, but they were not. They owned the fence I had driven through before nailing the left side of my Acadia to the tree. They waited with me for the ambulance. When the paramedics arrived, I was able to walk to the ambulance, mostly complaining about the searing pain in my right hand.

Jamie met me at the ER, while Molly stayed with our young kids and got them off to school. I left the hospital with a mild concussion diagnosis and a shattered hand, and surgery was quickly scheduled for early the following week. I navigated opening my first business with broken bones—almost all of them in my hand—and my first surgery. Fortunately, Molly was there for me, sitting with me when I experienced some of the worst pain of my life postsurgery and reassuring me that the gym would still open as planned.

Writing this story feels like I am writing about someone else's dramatic event. I now know I should have paused to take the time and energy to recover fully in the aftermath of the accident, but I am thankful I had a good friend to help me make it through, doing the best I could at the time. We stayed on the timeline due to the perseverance of friends and family, and especially Jamie, and renovated the gym at the end of December. We opened the Zone, as planned, on January 2, 2011. I taught group exercise with my hand elevated, and eventually everything settled into normality. Molly, who always claimed she didn't enjoy exercise, ended up working as a personal trainer and finishing a triathlon, and still loves to ride her bike today. We eventually went our separate ways professionally, but our families are still wonderful friends, spending most weekends together and traveling each year. I will always be thankful for her faith in me.

I learned that sharing your belief in others always matters. You might be the one to help them begin to truly believe anything is possible.

My friendship with Sadie started in 2009, when we were parent volunteers at our kids' preschool. We shared brief small talk, and through this connection and happenstance I was fortunate to be her trainer and eventual triathlon coach. Sadie initially inspired me with her independence and strong will. Our multifaceted friendship allowed for many honest conversations in which Sadie has challenged me, helped me grow, and modeled a spirit of strength. In 2017, after mentoring her for years, evolving our friendship, and training along-side her, watching her cross the Ironman finish line will forever be a highlight of my coaching career.

I learned that I can be myself and trust that others can as well.

My friendship with Kelli started a little differently but is built on a foundation of honesty. Kelli and I met when she came into the gym looking for a trainer, referred by a high school friend. We shared the experience of having three kids in a very tight time frame and immediately connected. Kelli told me that she was "not interested in running races or anything of that nature. She was there to get fit and lose weight." Over time we had more and more vulnerable conversations that led Kelli to share with me some traumatic events from her younger life. We became friends outside the gym, and eventually I convinced Kelli to run a 5K. Then I decided to challenge her further by giving her a race entry into the local 20K, offering to coach her and then run the race along-side her. I presented this gift at a party that we attended with many other members of the Zone. She did not anticipate my gift, and while a bit drunk, responded by kicking me. And I did not like it. The next day I sent Kelli an email telling her that I really liked her and wanted to be her friend and was more than willing to forgive her. But I also made it clear I was not okay with that kind of treatment in any of my relationships, even if regarded as playful. I am thankful that Kelli carefully considered my message, apologized, and told me friends had never called her out on that behavior before. And maybe her friends hadn't really been bothered by her intensity, but I was happy I could be completely honest with her. She is still one of my best friends today, and although our friendship has changed, it has always evolved on a foundation of mutual honesty and respect. I also had the honor to coach her to a goal she never thought possible and cheered her on with tears as she crossed the Ironman finish line in 2017.

I learned to see people for who they are and to trust that honesty begets honesty and connection.

Another amazing friend I have had the honor of connecting with is Bella. Bella came into my life in 2015 as my new pastor's wife. I had never befriended my pastor's wife before, and I had no intention of starting with Bella. As our church prepared for our new pastor, I was made aware that he and Bella were looking for a gym in their new home of Oregon, Wisconsin. So I asked Kelli if I could offer them a free membership at the Zone. She agreed—generosity has always been a strong value for her—and they started attending classes. I was very drawn to Brandy's work ethic, goofy sense of humor, and obvious love for people. I thought she was cool. Then Brandy tried to befriend me beyond her role in the church. I was interested, but I was still stinging from the end of my confusing friendships with Katie and Ella. I was ready to invest further in my current friends and take a break from risking new friendships, so I bluntly told Bella that we could be friends but only on the acquaintance level. She could enter one of the outer friendship circles, but I wanted her to be aware that I wasn't taking any applications to get into the smaller, tighter circles that were closer to my heart and required more of my time and energy.

Fortunately, Bella was persistent. She gave me space to hold my boundary but still initiated times to get together. As I got to know her more, I looked forward to our insightful, thought-provoking, real conversations. Our shared value of faith became a sturdy foundation that we could build on with a level of understanding. Bella helped ease my pain and frustration about the failure of past friendships and guided my pendulum back to the center. She reminded me that honesty is important, but I must learn to better deliver it as truth *and* love. I was able to overcome my bitterness and stop fixating on the idea of being right instead focusing on loving.

My friendship with Bella continues to grow, and while she reminded me of the person I truly desire to be, I was able to see her in her imperfect realness. I had encouraged her in the past to teach group exercise because her excitement for fitness and competition is infectious. She became a valued instructor and trainer at the Zone and continued to train with the new company when it was sold, and now owns her own business and is a health coach for church workers. Our foundation of honesty and trust provided an environment where we could work together to overcome her deep-seated phobia of swimming. In 2018 Bella became a triathlete and—I'm sure—will someday be an Ironman. She still amazes and teaches me today.

I learned to stay open and vulnerable to new relationships, or you could miss one of the best.

My friend Elizabeth is an amazing force, physically strong and determined. She asks good questions, and although we agree on much, she also challenges me to think differently. She is mentally and emotionally open to giving all herself to others as a part-time social worker for the county. She loves animals and cares for what we like to refer to as a "zoo" at her home. Elizabeth and her husband, Aaron, inspire me in a unique way to many people in my life. They remind me to be present and to have fun. They are smart, committed friends who love to have thought-provoking conversations and debates, but at the soul level, they are lovers, hippies, and faithful friends who would drop everything to help any creature.

Years ago, Aaron surprised our friend circle by announcing he had quit his job as a banker. He had received a severance, but he had no job lined up. Although none of my business, I found it hard to not reflect on how I felt about his decision. He was the main breadwinner in their family, and because I love him, Elizabeth, and their three amazing kids, I wanted them to be okay. After talking with Elizabeth and Aaron and understanding that they weren't going to lose everything, I was nothing less than inspired.

My relationship with such friends reminds me that sometimes you have to make tough choices out of a strong desire for more joy in life.

I am so thankful for the value they bring to my life and for the laughs and amazing memories we have and will continue to make, in all aspects of life, including training and racing.

I am also very privileged to have had my most dedicated support at home. Jamie and my three young adult children have consistently given me space and encouragement to be the best I can be. We have had many ups, downs, obstacles, and roadblocks. We have cycled through codependence, interdependence, and independence. We have all evolved, yet we still desire to be together. When I tell them my race goals, they don't doubt my abilities. When I told them I was writing a book, they showed visible excitement. I don't need their validation, but it does feel good to receive it from those I love most. And I don't give them the credit for reaching my goals, but my life is richer, fuller, and sincerely better with them by my side. They inspire me and force me to be better by practicing what I preach. I believe relationships help shape you, and I am honored to have the four of them closest to me for life. Hopefully, you have the same good fortune, but if not, build your "family of choice" around your passions so that you can draw on their support.

HOW YOU CAN LEARN FROM ME

- Acknowledge and celebrate strong friendship bonds. Surround yourself with people who believe in you and tell them you believe in them. Engage with close friends who challenge you, not merely enable you.

- Consider how having healthy bonds contributes to your goal setting and actualizing. Having support is important to leading a real, full life. Seek out these relationships, and/or be grateful for the good in those that you have.

HAVE FUN!

It is my sincere hope that the takeaway from this book is not that you have to take on every single goal in your life with the purpose of going hard, fast, or with tunnel-vision focus. My desire is that you learn to have a well-defined purpose that you can return to in order to be content with the processes and outcomes. I hope you will learn to be open to the many lessons in life and have enough amazing people to help guide and teach you. Life is not always fun, happy, or easy, but it often does not have to be as complicated as we make it.

I can identify many different kinds of fun, from working hard to reach goals to peeing your pants with goofy laughter to going out dancing until 4:00 a.m., among many, many other activities. I have had the most fun in the moments of life when I know the sole purpose is just that—*to have fun*. These moments might have yielded fewer awards or accolades, but the memories of the laughter, joy, and connection will always be worth it.

I have also had fun accomplishing goals when the priority purpose has been to be the encourager of others. In 2010 my amazing high school friend Leslie asked me to run a marathon with her. I had run two open marathons at this point, my first being a total disaster on a shockingly hot October day in Wisconsin in 2007, and my second being a strong comeback in Green Bay in the spring of 2008. I love Leslie and eagerly agreed to put my own interests on the back burner to help a lifelong friend achieve her goal. Unfortunately, during the process of training, I acquired an overuse injury in my knee. I tried to rest, back off on my mileage, and do all that I could to get to the starting line alongside my friend. Luckily, I had a clear vision for my purpose of this race, which was to have fun encouraging someone else, and so I wasn't fighting the desire to perform. I was able to compromise with myself and Leslie—I would be the biggest cheerleader for the first sixteen miles of the race and then hop in for the final and most challenging ten. Our plan worked. It was fun, and she proudly finished her first marathon.

I believe a big part of my purpose is not only to inspire through personal actions but also to encourage others to live as their best selves. As a coach and supportive friend, I have had the joyous experience of encouraging others for many race goals. I have had the opportunity to give back to the people who have taught me so much by believing in them and then literally running alongside them to ignite the spark of their own fiery confidence. I have enjoyed the role of coach and supporter numerous times on the sidelines and found the fun in participating for others through charity events. I have coached hundreds of young people over ten years with the goal of having fun while completing the Oregon Kids Triathlon, a local race that nearly every young athlete in our small town has participated in at least once. Leading, working with, and helping prepare those kids is fun—well, most of the time—and it will always be one of my favorite days of the year. My face hurts from smiling after it is done.

I have been fortunate to take many girls on race trips, with the very obvious purpose of having fun in Miami, New Orleans, and Key West. These races were the most fulfilling when I focused on the specific purpose of the race and the trip—to have fun. Early on in these experiences, I would sometimes let the thoughts of personal records and performance muddle my intentions, causing the undue stress of *purpose confusion.* This occurs when you misalign your why and end up chasing two opposing goals. When I settled into the real purpose for each goal I set, I was able to fully enjoy the moment with a true sense of accomplishment.

Jamie and I have also completed two Tough Mudder obstacle courses and other fun mud runs. Like Aaron and Elizabeth, these races reminded me of the fun in life. We still had to train and work toward the goals, but it was more about the joy of working together than it was about competition. Although there were glimpses of competitive purpose confusion, I focused on letting go of that in the moment to enjoy the time with my friends and team. I believe I am retired from mud runs, especially the ones where they give you an electric shock at the end, but I am very thankful for the memories. These goals were set with the clear purpose of working together to have fun.

HOW YOU CAN LEARN FROM ME

- Live each moment to honor the reason and avoid purpose confusion. You can work hard and have fun but understand how work and fun fit together.
- Create close relationships with friends who will ask for help and give you the gift of being the "encourager."
- Have fun!

CONCLUSION

GOING FURTHER

*Fight for the things that you care about, but do it in a way that will
lead others to join you.*
RUTH BADER GINSBURG

FAR BETTER IS A COLLECTION OF MANY OF THE LESSONS I HAVE
LEARNED *SO FAR*. I excitedly anticipate continuing to learn through
and alongside the power of endurance sports. In the time it took for
me to write this book, I have experienced several shifts and changes
professionally and in relationships and have learned new things. The
fantastic thing about life is that as I have already moved on, the lessons
I learned are enduring.

Nothing is perfect in my life, and I still live in a reactive or victim
state at times. I have default ways of thinking; can be snarky, impa-
tient, and judgmental, among many other negative qualities; and I

fall into bad habits. But I try to be honest with myself and others.

The most recent world events have taught me so much about who I am and how important it is to reach people with the message to care for themselves to better serve others. I will never have all the answers, but I will do my part to keep learning and to stand up against injustice. I will keep seeking out ways to be more connected to my purpose of mentoring, inspiring, and supporting athletes to dig deep and learn more through racing and be able to apply it to their entire lives, including their athletic endeavors. I am committed to searching deeper within to explore how I can further motivate others to live out their purpose and positively contribute to the greater good. I have done this hard work to create awareness in myself not so I can arrive at a finish line but so that I can go forth better serving others, which I believe is what my faith and intuition tell me is the essence of a meaningful life.

I have lived an amazing life so far. My life fully blossomed when I honored my goal of adding writing into my daily practice. I still love to train and race, and my life's work will always involve coaching and inspiring in some way, but I sincerely felt for many years that becoming a writer was something I had needed to do to honor myself. Although I do not see the deadly COVID-19 pandemic as a gift, I am thankful for life slowing down so that I could have the headspace to let go of the fears surrounding writing and have the clarity of mind to understand that I really only ever wanted to do this for myself— that you are reading this is a wonderful added bonus.

As a parting message, I encourage you to get interested in your own life. Connect with and get to know yourself. See your strengths and your flaws. Feel the negativity. Give in to the beauty of caring for yourself so that you can fully share your abilities and talents with others. Find a snazzy vehicle, get in the driver seat, and set off on the road to finding and celebrating your own passion and purpose. And if you decide to race, do it with joy and gratitude. You will never know when a race will be your last.

Cheers,

MB

HOW YOU CAN LEARN FROM ME: A WORKBOOK

I see your fear, and it's big. I also see your courage, and it's bigger.
We can do hard things.
GLENNON DOYLE, *UNTAMED*

EXERCISE 1: THIS IS WHO I AM AND WHO I WILL BECOME

Take the time to really consider your answers—this is a chance for you to get to know you!

I am [insert your personal and professional roles]:

....

....

....

....

....

I am a dreamer. I dream about:

I am passionate about:

I am strong. My strengths are [name at least three]:

I am not perfect. Some of my weaknesses are [name at least three]:

I am unique. One of my quirks is:

I am always changing. Right now, I like [name at least three things]:

And I dislike [name at least three things]:

I am patient. Something I tolerate often is:

Something I just can't tolerate is:

I will continue to do great things. A short-term life goal is to:

I have a short-term physical goal of:

I will keep growing. Right now, I have a long-term life goal of:

_____

_____

_____

_____

A long-term physical goal is to:

_____

_____

_____

_____

I know my purpose. Right now, my purpose in life is:

_____

_____

_____

_____

I will continue to live out my purpose by:

_____

_____

_____

_____

_____

_____

_____

_____

_____

_____

_____

EXERCISE 2: SETTING DAILY INTENTIONS

Although we cannot always control the circumstances of our lives, we can control how we react. Each day you have the opportunity to make choices that contribute to your well-being. Set daily intentions to increase mindfulness throughout your day.

- Sit down for at least ten minutes each morning and journal your intentions for the day.
- Write two intentions for the day that will honor you in this moment and also your why.
- Return to these often during the day, especially when you want to make self-destructive choices or are struggling, uncomfortable, needing to make tough decisions, and so on.
- Practice self-compassion if you fail to honor your best intentions. Reflect and learn from the experience and give yourself grace before moving on to the next daily practice.

EXERCISE 3: FIND YOUR WHY

Why is knowing your why so important?

It is important to have an overarching why or purpose and then to set individual whys for each goal. Knowing both of these will serve as your point of reference for all your actions and decisions regarding your life and individual goals. Doing so will also allow you to measure your progress. It will prioritize your goal as a form of honoring and caring for yourself and your needs. Basically, it will help you get up day after day, even when it is hard or you don't want to, and consider how you can make progress toward purpose and your individual goals.

Your why statements should:

- honor your core values,
- be simple and clearly actionable, and
- have a purposeful connection to all humanity.

A simple formula: *I value [insert values], and so I will [insert overarching or individual/short-term intention] in order to [insert impact on others]*.

For example, my overarching why: I value growth, health, and overall well-being, and so I will inspire and encourage others through words and actions to set hard goals, to grow, and to learn in order to be the best version of themselves, not only as athletes but as people.

My current why for my next endurance race goal: I value hard work and integrity, and so I will show up to my Ironman Saint George training process daily in order to encourage and inspire my family, friends, athletes, readers, and social media followers that we can find value in doing hard things.

Your overarching why:

A why for a current/short-term goal:
(*Find Your Why* by Simon Sinek is an amazing resource on this topic.)

EXERCISE 4: CAPTURING YOUR THOUGHTS

How do you think about yourself? Do you think you have a healthy daily thought life?

Do you believe you are capable of doing what it takes to reach your goals?

How to "Capture" Your Thoughts

It is eye-opening (and exhausting!) to focus on our thoughts for one day. And just thinking it truly doesn't make it "true." Take three times out of the day to focus on and "capture" your thoughts for one hour in the morning, midday, or evening. Practice this during normal life activities (this is not meditation), and jot down as many as you can remember. *Do not* judge thoughts as "bad" or "good" or try to distract yourself from perceived negative thoughts.

When you have captured a thought, ask yourself the following questions:

Why do I think this?

Is it true?

What makes it true?

Practicing this often will help you more deeply investigate your mind while your emotional response is lower. This exercise reduces the tendency to blame others and to have an attitude of victimization, helping you be more accepting of negativity and be more present overall. It also has the potential to help you perceive your goals differently.

EXERCISE 5: SELF-EFFICACY, SELF-CONFIDENCE, AND SELF-ESTEEM

Self-efficacy is a person's belief in their ability to succeed in a particular situation. Your journey toward goal actualization begins with this belief.

Different scales are used to evaluate levels of self-efficacy, including the General Self-Efficacy Scale (GSE) and the Self-Efficacy Questionnaire. For a quick, informal assessment of your own self-efficacy levels, consider the following questions:

Do you feel like you can handle problems if you are willing to work hard?

Are you confident in your ability to achieve your goals?

Do you feel like you can manage unexpected events that come up?

Are you able to bounce back quickly after stressful events?

Do you feel you can come up with solutions when you are facing a problem?

Do you keep trying, even when things seem difficult?

Are you good at staying calm, even in the face of chaos?

Do you perform well under pressure?

Can you focus on your progress, even when overwhelmed by all you still have to do?

_____
_____
_____
_____

Do you believe that hard work will eventually pay off?

_____
_____
_____
_____

How does your self-efficacy rate?

_____
_____
_____
_____
_____

How can you improve your self-efficacy?

_____
_____
_____
_____
_____
_____

Setting goals is crucial to building your self-efficacy. Set small and measurable goals, ensuring that the process toward reaching them is out of your comfort zone. Learn from failures rather than dwell on them. Don't let them break your self-trust. Basically, cultivate awareness and keep practicing all you have learned!

Note your plan here:

SELF-ESTEEM ASSESSMENT

Life is too short to spend it not being the truest version of you! You are wonderfully made and worthy of love. Bringing awareness to and, if needed, improving your self-confidence will lead to achieving your best.

What is self-confidence?
Self-confidence is the trust you have in your own abilities, capacities, judgments, or beliefs to be able to successfully face daily challenges or demands. Self-confidence is more based on past performances than self-efficacy.

What is self-esteem?

Self-esteem is how much you appreciate and like yourself. Your self-esteem is more of a personality trait, which often makes it more stable and enduring and therefore harder to change.

Task: Review the Rosenberg self-esteem scale. You can find this scale at: www.wwnorton.com/college/psych/psychsci/media/rosenberg.htm.

Note your results here:

How does your perception of your self-esteem compare to the results of the scale?

Can you identify someone or something in your life that helped shape your self-esteem?

If desired, how do you plan to improve your self-esteem?

Is there a goal you would like to take on if you improved your self-efficacy, confidence, and/or self-esteem?

Why does this matter, and how can you work toward loving and believing in yourself?

_____

_____

_____

_____

_____

_____

_____

Typically, when you are more self-confident in your abilities, you see your successes and celebrate them more. Also, when you are feeling better about your capabilities, the more energized and motivated you are to take action and achieve your goals.

If you decide you cannot do something before you even try, then you make an excuse based on that judgment, not on your true possible physical and mental capabilities. You shrink your comfort zone.

EXERCISE 6: SELF-TRUST

Self-trust is vital in cultivating a better relationship with ourselves, which leads to improved self-confidence and efficacy.

Do you trust yourself?

_____

_____

_____

_____

_____

_____

Indicate what you feel is true from the following list of signs that point to a lack of trust in oneself:

- I have a hard time recognizing, understanding, or believing in my own innate value and worth.
- I do things to prove my value to myself and others.
- I try to control everything around me so that I can feel safe.
- I compare the choices I have made to those made by others.
- I minimize or deny my own needs.
- It's sometimes difficult to recognize or tell the truth to myself and/or others.
- I am unable or unwilling to challenge my self-sabotaging or self-destructive thoughts, beliefs, and behavior patterns.
- I participate in self-sabotaging or compulsive behaviors that create shame, guilt, or self-punishment.
- I break the promises I have made to myself.

- I find it difficult to finish what I start.
- I hold in anger, resentment, or ill will toward—or I speak negatively about—those who I feel have hurt or harmed me.
- I deny or minimize my power of choice.
- I defer to others, allowing them to make choices and decisions for me.
- I feel that I am always reacting rather than living intentionally.
- I rely heavily on my physical senses and am often disconnected from my intuition, instincts, and inner guidance.

After indicating what you find to be true, spend some quiet time reflecting on your answers. Consider your level of self-trust again. And then see below on how to improve.

How can you go forward working toward building trust for yourself and learn to follow your intuition more?

- Learn who you are and then be that person. Surround yourself with people who allow you to be you.
- Spend quiet time with yourself. Meditate. Practice mindfulness to boost self-knowledge. Plan downtime.
- Make decisions without looking for guidance from others. Be decisive.
- Be kind to yourself. Have grace and forgiveness for you.
- Set reasonable goals and spend some time in your strengths. Be present in the moment and focus on gratitude for what you are good at.
- Listen to your body. Mindfully accept and let go of negative emotions.

Detail your plan toward more self-trust:

EXERCISE 7: FEAR IS A LIAR

Why is it important to acknowledge fear in goal setting?
We cannot ignore or hide from fear. The only way we can break through our fears is *through* them, not around, under, or over them. Fear thrives in the darkness and starts to diminish when exposed to the light, so when it comes to squashing fears and working toward big goals, you either make excuses or a plan. We cannot be vulnerable and connect with others while living with immense amounts of fear.

Why does fear hold us back?
Sometimes fears take form in a phobia, defined as "an extreme or irrational fear or aversion to something." Phobias are more deep-rooted and require more professional help to overcome than I can provide (although they can be overcome!), but there are some basic fears that don't fall into the phobia category that you can tackle. *Fear of failure and/or fear of change* are the two main obstacles to goal setting.

Fear of failure can manifest in many ways and is directly connected with insecurity. Some are obvious, such as not trying new things, making excuses, or belittling the goal or experience. Others are sneakier and can be masked as a "positive" trait, such as overscheduling, busyness, competitive behavior, and perfectionism.

Often connected to fear of failure, the fear of change can cause you to feel stuck in often unhealthy situations and circumstances. It can lead to loneliness and depression.

How can I stop fear being a force in my life?

The first step is considering what you really want and realizing that fear could be holding you back, acknowledging that this is not a worthy excuse or positive approach to life. Allow yourself to consider what it would feel like to change some of your fear-masking behaviors and possibly fail. Focus on your needs and not on how you perceive anyone else will think or how they will react.

Take the time and fill out the questions below. It is imperative that you focus on being *honest* with yourself. Don't silence your small voice, as we often do, to stay in control of what you *think* you want. Be bold!

Fear and Goal Setting

List all fears.

_____

_____

_____

_____

_____

_____

_____

_____

List the ways fear is holding you back. What are some of your behaviors that help you avoid feeling fear, specifically fear of failure?

_____

_____

_____

_____

_____

When you face a fear, do you typically make an excuse or make a plan? How will you recognize excuses and stop validating them?

List your priorities using your head (that is, what you *think* your priorities should be) and then using your heart (how can you honor yourself, your passion, and your core values). How do you and your goals fit on this list?

Tell someone you *trust* about your fears and your goals. Choose someone who will encourage you and hold you accountable, not enable past behavior. Note below how this interaction went.

EXERCISE 8: CORE VALUES

In order to know yourself fully, you must identify your core values. These are the things that are most important to you and the starting point for all major (and minor!) decisions.

List your top-five core values.

Name five people who inspire you and one to five of their core values. Aren't sure what their core values are? Ask them or give your best guess.

Name one to three past joyful experiences in life. Be completely honest and do not overthink or write down what you think these experiences should be. This is a vital part in you knowing and accepting who you are!

Name one to three past awful experiences in life. Same as above: be honest!

_____

_____

_____

_____

_____

_____

_____

_____

_____

Do you feel that you honor your core values when making decisions? How do you plan to do this more in the future?

_____

_____

_____

_____

_____

_____

_____

_____

_____

_____

_____

_____

_____

_____

_____

EXERCISE 9: SHAME AND THE COURAGE IN VULNERABILITY

In her book *Daring Greatly*, leading shame researcher Brené Brown defines *shame* as "the intensely painful feeling or experience of believing that we are flawed and therefore unworthy of love and belonging—something we've experienced, done, or failed to do makes us unworthy of connection."

Identify a time in your life where you felt large amounts of shame. How did you react to it? Did you use guilt positively in order to amend your behavior? Or did you use shame to blame, hide, and/or protect yourself? Write about it below.

We all have times when we feel shame. It takes courage to still show up and be vulnerable, especially when we feel beat down by shame. In *Daring Greatly*, Brené Brown describes *vulnerability* as "uncertainty, risk, and emotional exposure." It's that unstable feeling we get when we step out of our comfort zone or do something that forces us to loosen control.

Let's break down one past experience of shame and practice vulnerability this week:

What was the event about which you are ashamed? What triggered you to feel shame? Capture all your thoughts around this and write them down.

Do you find these thoughts to be true? Why? Investigate your thoughts while simultaneously focusing on being kind and patient with yourself. We truly all make mistakes!

How do you need to move forward with this situation? If you negatively affected someone else (for example, missing an appointment or deadline), do you need to make amends with them or with yourself? Who in your life can you tell about this situation, and how can you talk to them about it?

Did you have the opportunity to practice vulnerability in this experience? How? How did it feel?

Why this matters for goal setting: Identifying the difference between shame, guilt, embarrassment, and fear will aid in the process of allowing you to radically accept yourself. Being able to practice vulnerability with yourself and others will always be the first and most vital step in believing you can accomplish big goals. You must believe you can in order to take on the risks that matter to you, and then you can serve the world better!

EXERCISE 10: FEEL IT ALL

I believe in the idea that our thoughts control our feelings, and our feelings control our actions. When we experience negative emotions, our first line of defense is often to resist the feeling of the emotion, which makes the overall experience worse. The more we can practice *feeling*, the more we will live a full and content life without the fear of experiencing negative emotions. When we practice this in our daily life, we can experience the negative feelings that come along with the discomfort of setting challenging goals, disrupting our schedule, and training at high intensities.

Describe a time recently when you experienced a negative emotion (anxiety, fear, sadness, shame, and so on).

How did this feel in your body? How would you describe it to a stranger who has never heard of this emotion? Be specific.

Was the above difficult for you? Why?

How to more fully feel:

- Slow down to experience emotion. Breathe. If you are running from it, you will resist it. *Allow* it. *Be* with it. *Name* it. For example: "This is *fear*. I am experiencing *fear*."
- Decide how this feels in your body. Where do you feel it? What does it look like to you? Use as many adjectives as you can to describe this feeling.
- Don't distract yourself from it, avoid it, or move on from it quickly. Take the time to be with it and understand the thoughts that are causing this feeling.

After you practice fully feeling your day-to-day emotions, you will realize they don't have the same power over you—the power that *you* give them!

How can you apply this to training and racing?

This can apply to the training and racing process in several ways:

1. You will feel that anything is possible when you are unafraid of feeling the negative emotions associated with setting your big goals (the possibility of fear, rejection, failure, shame, and so on). Therefore, you will make goals that you *really want* and have a sound why to accomplish.

2. You will establish your goal (for this process, a physical goal) as a priority in your life and will not make excuses or distract yourself from reaching it. You will *make time* to train, even when you have to make sacrifices to do so.

3. When you get ready to conquer hard training, long workouts, and/or high-intensity exercises, you will be connected to your body. You will be able to identify the physical experience as something that is being created in your brain and be able to *accept* it and *be* with it rather than do all you can to distract yourself from it, which ironically takes energy! Basically, you will be able to experience pain and discomfort as it is and trust that it won't kill you or last forever.

4. You will generally be more in tune with your body and therefore able to use more energy for your athletic performance than resisting negativity. You will be generally freer!

Practical Application

For one week, use the space below to note every occasion when you take the time to slow down and feel your emotions—not all negative, positive as well! Be specific about how these feelings manifest and move through your body. In training, *name* the physical feelings. Try to not quickly distract yourself from them; be with these daily emotions and training feelings.

For example: "This is *discomfort*. But I am okay. I feel this *discomfort*, but I can persevere. I am choosing to feel *discomfort*. *Discomfort* comes with reaching for high goals."

EXERCISE 11: COMPARISON

Comparison often has a negative connotation, especially when regarding building self-confidence and/or working toward goal actualization. Theodore Roosevelt is quoted as saying, "Comparison is the thief of joy." But, sometimes comparison can be used for good. Explore how you use comparison.

How do you compare yourself to others?

_____

_____

_____

_____

_____

_____

_____

_____

_____

How do you feel that using comparison impacts you negatively?

_____

_____

_____

_____

_____

_____

_____

_____

_____

Describe a situation when comparison, perhaps in the form of healthy competition, inspired you.

Comparison can do a multitude of negative things, including:

- Distracting you from your purpose, causing you to lose sight of your goals.
- Tapping into your insecurities and creating negative thoughts toward yourself or others.
- Cultivating feelings of superiority.
- Breeding feelings of inferiority, making you wish others would fail so you can feel better about yourself.
- Creating an unrealistic environment where you strive for perfection and/or aim for a life you don't understand and possibly don't even want.

But comparison can also positively impact your ability to reach your goals. A few ways include:

- Giving you the perspective to appreciate your position in life.
- Inspiring you to reach for your own success.
- Aiding self-growth through self-evaluation.

Answer the following questions as honestly as possible. Take the time to really dig into your brain so you can start to turn those insecurities and negative comparisons into positive competition and inspiration.

Who do you compare yourself to on a daily or weekly basis? How does this make you feel?

_____

_____

_____

_____

_____

_____

_____

_____

_____

Who inspires you? How does this make you feel?

_____

_____

_____

_____

_____

_____

_____

_____

_____

_____

Who do you compete with? Is this a negative or positive process for you?

How can you use inspiration and competition to be a better athlete?

EXERCISE 12: MINDFULNESS AND VISUALIZATION

Merriam-Webster defines *mindfulness* as follows:

noun

1: the quality or state of being mindful

2: the practice of maintaining a nonjudgmental state of heightened or complete awareness of one's thoughts, emotions, or experiences on a moment-to-moment basis

also: such a state of awareness

Do you currently believe in the importance and power of practicing mindfulness? If yes, what are your current practices?

....

....

....

....

....

....

....

....

Merriam-Webster defines *visualization* as follows:

noun

1: formation of mental visual images

Visualization can be a practiced mindfulness used for sport. Instead of focusing on your awareness of the present moment, you put yourself into future or past situations in order to learn from the experiences, build confidence and self-efficacy, and practice success in your mind. Mindfulness and visualization both matter *so much* for athletic (and life) success.

Seven-Day Mindfulness Challenge: Take five to ten minutes twice a day (once in the morning and once in the evening) to sit quietly and focus on your breathing. Try to calm your mind and body. Be present and not rushed.

When the seven days are complete, assess your practice. Consider the potential benefits of continuing to take five to ten minutes each day. Apply what you learn to being present in all situations in life, including challenging physical endeavors.

Visualization Practice

1. Find a quiet space. Spend some time just breathing. Then choose one past experience or endurance event and put yourself back into it from start to finish. Aim to feel it, as it was. What did you learn?

2. Find a quiet space. Spend some time just breathing. Then choose an upcoming event and imagine yourself competing, from start to finish. Be *real* and *open* to your feelings. How did this go?

EXERCISE 13: REST

There is no such thing as overtraining, but there is such a thing as underrecovering. Of course, sleep is a major element of rest.

On a scale of one to ten, how would you rate your average sleep quality?

How many hours per night, on average, do you sleep?

How many hours of sleep do you think you need to function at your best?

Sleep is important for everyone, especially athletes. With a lack of sleep, not only are you asking more of your body but also your brain, since its function is lowered. Hormones are also imbalanced by a lack of sleep. Tiredness can undermine your physical capabilities and stamina, your ability to mentally strategize, and your emotional and hormonal ability to deal with negative feelings. Simply put, sleep is vital to actualizing goals and living a fulfilling life.

Sleep Hygiene Study

For three consecutive nights this week, follow all the guidelines for good sleep hygiene. At the end of the week, answer the following questions:

How did you sleep?

_____

_____

_____

_____

Did you notice any changes in how you felt?

_____

_____

_____

_____

How did your workouts feel?

_____

_____

_____

_____

Did you experience more mental or emotional clarity?

_____

_____

_____

_____

_____

_____

What were the barriers to practicing good sleep hygiene?

EXERCISE 14: RECOVERY

Rest is one (very important) part of recovery. Some other methods of recovery include stretching, massage and other body work, ice baths, nutrition, and so on.

Identify your practices for the following modes of recovery:

1. Stretching:

2. Other body work:

3. Nutrition (specific to recovery):

How could you improve your recovery strategy?

Recovery Strategy Task

For one week, take notes on how rested you feel. Include any indicators that could factor in (relating to sleep, conflicts at home or work, recovery practices, and so on). Practice *really* feeling in your body—don't just gloss over it in an effort to ignore or coat it with toxic positivity. Rest and recovery are vital for you to reach your goals.

EXERCISE 15: SHIFTING THE CULTURE

The hurdles to men and women in sports are established and maintained by all of us through cultural expectations. We need everyone involved to understand the burdens in order to make the changes.

Use these prompts to start to write down some ways that you are influenced and also how you can contribute to change.

Reflect on what you think a "good" parent is. Write these traits down. Inspect them for truth while considering how your upbringing and ingested societal norms helped shape your expectations. Which thought patterns can you change?

Do the same for food. What do you consider "good" and "bad" food? What kind of food is "clean?" How do you feel when you eat these kinds of foods? What do you think of others when you see them eating "bad food?" How do you think diet culture influences the way you see food and your body? When do you think you "deserve" to enjoy food? Do you agree with the fact that parents can only have space because they "need it?"

REFERENCES

STAY CURIOUS

Brown, Brené. *Daring Greatly: How the Courage to Be Vulnerable Transforms the Way We Live, Love, Parent, and Lead.* New York: Avery, 2012.

BE WHOLLY YOU

Sims, Stacy T. *Roar: How to Match Your Food and Fitness to Your Unique Female Physiology for Optimum Performance, Great Health, and a Strong, Lean Body for Life.* New York: Rodale Inc., 2016.

Cerrato, Javier, and Eva Cifre. "Gender Inequality in Household Chores and Work-Family Conflict." *Frontiers in Psychology* 9 (2018). https://doi.org/10.3389/fpsyg.2018.01330.

PART 2: GATHER TOOLS

Roosevelt, Franklin D. *Looking Forward.* New York: John Day Co., 1933.

KNOW WHY

Chin, Jimmy, and Elizabeth Chai Vasarhelyi. *Free Solo*. Little Monster Films, Itinerant Films, Parkes + MacDonald Image Nation, National Geographic Documentary Films, 2018.

TAKE CARE OF YOURSELF TO BETTER CARE FOR OTHERS

Doyle, Glennon. *Untamed*. New York: The Dial Press, 2020.

HOW YOU CAN LEARN FROM ME: A WORKBOOK

Sinek, S., David Mead, and Peter Docker. *Find Your Why: A Practical Guide for Discovering Purpose for You and Your Team*. New York: Portfolio, 2017.

Cherry, Kendra. "Self Efficacy and Why Believing in Yourself Matters," *Verywell Mind*, February 27, 2023, https://www.verywellmind.com/what-is-self-efficacy-2795954.

Rosenberg, Morris. *Society and the Adolescent Self-Image*. Princeton, NJ: Princeton University Press, 1965.

ABOUT THE AUTHOR

Miranda Bush is a USA Triathlon coach for Zone Racing, a triathlon team in her local community, as well as a certified health coach and strength coach. She owns MB Coaching and co-owns Zone Racing. Miranda is a longtime age-group triathlete, with multiple Ironman and 70.3 finishes, including many on the podium. She still races today—sometimes for fun and other times to compete, but always to learn firsthand how to be a more aware and inspiring coach, leader, and human.

Miranda studied English literature at the University of Wisconsin–Madison. You can also find her work in *Triathlete Magazine* online, at TrainingPeaks, and at Feisty Triathlon. She believes athletes can benefit from her story and expertise in a way that adds value to their racing careers and overall lives.

Miranda currently resides in Oregon, Wisconsin, with her husband, Jamie, and dogs, Jake and Bruce, while supporting her three college-aged kids. In addition to racing with her friends and family, she loves to read, travel, and be outside as much as possible.